The Zena Sutherland Lectures
1983-1992

To Russell Friedman
With gratitude for the many
outstanding books that
have given pleasure to
their readers,
including — affectionately
Zena Sutherland

The Zena Sutherland Lectures 1983-1992

Betsy Hearne, Editor

Clarion Books
New York

Clarion Books
a Houghton Mifflin Company imprint
215 Park Avenue South, New York, NY 10003
Text copyright © 1993 by The Zena Sutherland Lectureship Fund

Printed in the USA
Book design and typography by Carol Goldenberg

Library of Congress Cataloging-in-Publication Data
The Zena Sutherland lectures, 1983–1992 / Betsy Hearne, editor.
p.   cm.
ISBN 0-395-64504-2 (hardcover) 0-395-64987-0 (paperback)
1. Children—United States—Books and reading.
2. Children's literature, American—History and criticism.
I. Sutherland, Zena.   II. Hearne, Betsy Gould.
Z1037.Z46   1993
011.62—dc20   92-29781   CIP

BP 10 9 8 7 6 5 4 3 2 1

Contents

Introduction

ON THE EVENING OF January 19, 1980, John Donovan, Sophie Silberberg, Bob Verrone, Dorothy Briley, and Marilyn Kaye gathered at my house to have dinner and to discuss a person who ordinarily would have been part of the party: Zena Sutherland. We were planning a festschrift in honor of her outstanding career in the field of children's literature, which Sophie Silberberg detailed so eloquently in an introduction to the book that resulted from our midwinter conspiracy: *Celebrating Children's Books: Essays on Children's Literature in Honor of Zena Sutherland.* One of the greatest tributes to Zena's work, both as editor of the *Bulletin of the Center for Children's Books* for twenty-seven years and as professor of children's literature at the University of Chicago's Graduate Library School, was the unanimously positive response of all twenty-two writers, artists, and critics who were asked to contribute essays to the festschrift. (The hardest part was keeping it a secret from Zena.) The royalties for *Celebrating Children's Books,* a 1981 publication that Marilyn Kaye and I edited with the help of Dorothy Briley, have gone to the Sutherland Lectureship Fund, which supports an annual presentation by a distinguished figure in the field of children's literature. The fund has increased with generous gifts from alumni, publishers, and several anonymous donors.

Sadly, three beloved members of that advisory committee for the festschrift have died: Bob Verrone in 1984, Sophie Silberberg in 1991, and John Donovan in 1992. Each was creative in many ways, but their common talent was friendship. They would have been deeply happy to celebrate the tenth anniversary of the Sutherland Lectures.

The Sutherland Lecture Committee, which includes Hazel Rochman, Isabel McCaul, Roger Sutton, Betsy Hearne, Elizabeth Huntoon as chair, and Zena herself to keep us all on track, has shaped and served the lecture series from its beginning. Each member has helped in some unique way, but Liz Huntoon's coordination of the lectureship with the Chicago Public Library has been a special labor of love that bridges academic and professional communities. It was my privilege to introduce the speakers every year except the first, when Boyd Rayward, then dean of the Graduate Library School, launched the series with a warm acknowledgment of the achievements of both Zena Sutherland and the first lecturer, Maurice Sendak. Boyd's notes are long lost somewhere between Chicago and Australia, where he's now professor of librarianship at the University of New South Wales. Fortunately, Maurice needs no introduction, nor do the other speakers who followed him, but it became part of the celebratory tradition.

These first ten lectures, given from 1983 to 1992, involved a stellar cast: Maurice Sendak, Lloyd Alexander, Katherine Paterson, Virginia Hamilton, Robert Cormier, Paula Fox, David Macaulay, Jean Fritz, Trina Schart Hyman, and Betsy Byars. Seven of the lecturers had already participated in the festschrift but were generous enough to share further with an audience that gathered eagerly for the Sutherland Lecture every year. The subjects, left to the choice of each lecturer, have ranged from fantasy to realism, from Chinese history to the African American experience, from creating picture books to capturing the excitement of technological information. While the quality of the lectures has been consistently high, the tone has varied with that element of surprise which distinguishes any real work of art. Maurice Sendak's ingeniously free-associated anecdotes provide an informal counterweight to Paula Fox's precise consideration of words; the contrast between Katherine Paterson's deeply rooted concern for social issues and Betsy Byars's exploration of what children find funny makes lively reading.

One of the collection's revealing aspects is the power of story to communicate more memorably than the most carefully rendered description or exposition. Of all the points made here, those contained in stories have the strongest impact. What is intelligent and moving finds its most durable expression in stories. These ten writers and artists are, above all, great storytellers in one medium or another. Their skill is evidence of the important contribution children's literature can make to our lives: the perpetuation of story as a mind-saver in the midst of senseless, often senselessly tragic, circumstances. Those who can tell, draw, dance, sing, act, or play a story restore to the universe some sense of pattern which the human spirit craves.

That librarians have championed storytelling in person and in print represents a visionary, and largely unacknowledged, act in our culture; that universities are closing library schools shows how little that vision is valued. The closing of the Graduate Library School at the University of Chicago was reprehensible, but it has revealed bits of truth, among them the fact that individuals can succeed where institutions fail. The book that was inspired by Zena Sutherland, that was edited by her students, that was composed by writers and artists whom she encouraged through perceptive criticism—that book has reached a wide circle of listeners and has engendered another book, the one you are about to read. A good story grows with the telling.

Betsy Hearne, July 20, 1992

The
Zena Sutherland
Lectures
1983-1992

Maurice Sendak

Sources of Inspiration
May 20, 1983

I WANT TO BEGIN by saying how pleased I am to have been chosen to inaugurate this series of lectures in honor of Zena Sutherland. Zena and I are old friends, and that — considering the looniness of the publishing profession in general and the perfect madness of children's books in particular — is no small feat. We gossip and cackle together, increasingly worry about the state of publishing, and have even been known to mourn over the good old days.

I asked Zena for a particular favor this evening, and I knew she'd be happy to grant it: we are dedicating this first Sutherland lecture to the memory of our good friend Ezra Jack Keats, who died two weeks ago. Ezra, Zena, and I — and some few other favorite colleagues — grew up in the business together. Ezra's death brought sharply back those good old days — the golden 1950s and 1960s of children's book publishing in America. They are not only golden in retrospect; they were golden to us then. We were the postwar generation in publishing, and we knew and felt the exceptional time that we lived in. Craftsmanship was taken for granted; the ingredients that composed a book were of the highest quality, a reaction, certainly, to the very low quality that we had had to endure during the Second World War.

In a sense, we reinvented the picture book. It was an extraordinary time to be young and to be an artist in America. Most of us were baptized into adulthood by psychoanalysis — you just didn't make it in the 1950s unless you went through therapy — and everywhere there was an exciting and revived interest in children: their language, the state of their minds and hearts. Best of all, children's books had not yet grown into a prosperous and competing business. There was little money to be made and lots of time for a young artist to apprentice himself to the publishing and printing craft and grow up in an industry that, for the most part, had very high ideals.

Ezra's death, for me, spotlights that very brief time in history. His work represents the highest in craft and quality; he was one of us lucky kids. Those times are mostly gone, but I don't want to sadden my tribute to an old friend by becoming depressing and typically middle-aged about what is lost. There are beginning signs of fresh new life in publishing; I think it bodes well for the future, which brings me to my theme.

My theme for this evening, happily, is sources of inspiration. I say *happily* because the subject connotes chaos and natural disorder, thus allowing me, in truth to that subject, to deliver a fairly chaotic and disorderly lecture. There are many visions of the creative act. I endorse the romantic vision, as opposed to the cool vision endorsed by cool artists who seat themselves in front of a typewriter and coolly tap out chapter one, even chapter two, before lunch. I see the creative act as a vast nothingness, and the muse is the only one who is ever out to lunch. It is a void into which you fearfully hurl yourself, hoping at best not to break all your bones. So, how to speak of sources of inspiration? I think rather, as you will see, in a stream-of-consciousness manner; in my case, only connecting what may seem disparate elements — bits and pieces of conscious and even unconscious memory forcibly brought to the surface — that have guided me for a lifetime. Some of those have led me down a dead-end, and others, I hope, to an illumination of the self and to insights into that grand and terrifying and mostly uncivilized country called childhood.

I am going to illustrate my theme with two, maybe more, anecdotes which for me strongly suggest the flavor of that mysterious creative process, those murky sources of inspiration. But I will preface those anecdotes with a repeat of my definition of the creative process. Why a repeat? Because for me, "murky sources" made me think of muddy water, and that, perhaps, best describes the unconscious. I suggested earlier the image of broken bones; I think drowning is a better metaphor. I don't want to turn off young artists with all these sinister implications, but to be an artist is, of course, to be titillated by dangerous moments.

When you're searching sources, it's very much like throwing yourself into an ocean without an oxygen mask (there's something intoxicatingly suicidal about the creative process). You scoop up what looks like gold from the muddy floors only to see it transformed — mostly — to sludge in the cold light. There is always a measure of disappointment accompanying the search for inspiration, but there is also an immense sense of satisfaction and, occasionally, heroism. All these emotions balance art and, with work, keep artists from developing into complete egomaniacs. In all that ocean sludge, there are bits of gold that become the themes of all one's work — that are, in fact, the original sources of inspiration mostly lost, or rather hidden, in the encapsulated childhood world still living intact inside all of us. The creative process is intoxicating; it has the quality, or we pretend it does, of a life-and-death drama. It makes all the rest of living a fairly bleak business.

But I am going to move to an anecdote now, about something I saw on the streets of New York. I don't know why it affected me as deeply as it did, and it may sound very trivial, but it seems to me this is how vision must begin — this is what happened to William Blake one day.

I was walking down Fifth Avenue; it was a very beautiful day, which is rare for New York — a crystal-blue sky — and a man ran by, jogging, of course. Oddly, though, this particular person had a baby strapped to his back. He was obviously a young father, because he hadn't strapped the baby in well. I became very alarmed; he was busy doing his *shtick,* and the baby's head was, as babies' heads will, lumping back and forth like a giant watermelon. Terrified eyes, furrowed brow, mouth pulled down, desperate anxiety, but best keep still — even the baby knew that — and I really felt angry, like I should stop this fool before he killed his baby or brain-damaged it in some way. Anyhow, he went on and then came to a stop because the light had changed, and he stopped abruptly. Of course, the baby didn't know he was going to stop; the baby didn't even know why he was out in the street, doing this sort of torturous thing. He stopped so abruptly that the baby's head (and we all know babies' heads) fell back completely.

I was horrified, but God protects babies from such parents; we all know that. His face fell way back, and he stared straight up, quite gratuitously. He didn't know any of this was going to happen, and I watched him, and his face broke like a giant fruit into this enormous grin.

Now, I was thinking fast — *What's happening? What's happening?* — in a state of alarm, a state of distress. Suddenly this thing appears — he hasn't been taught that it's called *sky*, he doesn't know it's called *blue*, but it's wonderful, and it's an incredible relief from the torture he's been through, and it comes out of the blue, literally. His face was a revelation. And then I thought of William Blake, and I thought, *That's why William Blake saw angels.* Some horrible thing was happening, and his head fell down a certain way, and he saw something — white blossoms on a tree or whatever. It seemed surely that *blue* and *sky* would be imprinted on this baby's mind forever, and that somehow or other, all through his life, he was going to look up and feel better, and not have me to tell him why, that his silly-ass father did this to him. Well, then the light changed, and they went on, and that was the end of the vision. But it seemed this had to be a source of inspiration.

I associate this baby story immediately with an original baby story of my own. It pertains somewhat to an actual event in my life which happened when I was a baby, which I don't remember, but which had an effect on me. When I was writing and illustrating my last book, *Outside Over There,* I was fumbling for words. Anybody here who is a writer knows how you fumble for words — and you don't know what is the correct word, or why; why do you fight for the particular word? Why, when you catch it, is it the right word? Who's there to tell you there's a right or a wrong word? Well, there was a sentence in it: ". . . and Mama in the arbor." Now, I had Mama in every imaginable place for about six months, and it was all wrong; it just was not right. And then *arbor* came — and *arbor* had come very early on and I had rejected it as though it had come too fast, so I didn't trust it. When, after many weeks, I found myself back with *arbor,* it felt like giving in to a sensuous pleasure, like I had wanted *arbor* all the time. I had gone through mountains, streams, valleys, houses, porches, and all the rest. So it was *arbor,* and it stayed *arbor.* Long after *Outside Over There* was done — and I never show my work to anyone except my editor — my sister, who took both pleasure and grief from that book since she is nine years my senior and was the "Ida" in my life (she had much to complain about after she read it), made a particular point of coming to that line and, glowing, said, "Arbor, *Arbor.*"

I thought she was demented. I said, "What is it about *arbor?*" She said, "How can you remember such a thing?" I said, "I don't remember such a thing." Then she related something, much like this baby and his jogging papa, that presumably had much the same effect on me, which was that we lived in Brooklyn, and she cared for me — as I said, she was nine years older than I, so she was stuck with me — and she wheeled me about (I had heard most of that), and during those hot summer days we lived in a neighborhood made up of immigrant Jewish and Sicilian families, and her best friend was Rosanna, a Sicilian girl who lived down the street.

In those early days — this was the late twenties, early thirties — there were farms, and the Sicilian farmers came and set up their farms right there in the streets of Brooklyn. I remember some of them as I grew up. Well, it seems that on those very hot days, my sister would wheel me, that cranky, noisy baby that she told me frequently I was, to Rosanna's house. Rosanna's father had an arbor where he grew grapes. And she said, "The only way you would shut up was that I would wheel you into the arbor and I'd leave you there, and Rosanna and I would go and play movie games where she was Clark Gable and I was Janet Gaynor, and we'd use you if we needed a baby in the movie, but for the most part, we'd forget about you if we could." And she said, "It was the most extraordinary thing that you would shut up *instantly* on being wheeled into the arbor. Not a sound would come out of you, and if we looked at you, you had this immense grin on your face."

All I could think was that suddenly, after looking at her tiresome face, the vision was changed overhead. Natalie was gone, and leaves appeared, and great clumps of marvelous-smelling fruit. It must have had an enormous effect on me; I probably hated it when she wheeled me out of the arbor. But in fact, I wonder — and of course there's no way of proving it — did that memory so charge me up that, forty-five (or more) odd-years later, I am writing a book, and the word is almost an aphrodisiac? I have to use it, and yet I repress the urge to use it, and then I use it, and there, in fact, is Mama in the arbor. Well, make of it what you will, but I believe — and I'm a cynical man — that we do recollect these things from the time we were babies. I don't know how we do it. There's some fabulous machinery in there; we know about this fabulous machinery that takes care of such memories, but how it distills them and gives them back to us, that we don't know.

Let me tell you another source for *Outside Over There*. Some will hardly call this inspiration, but rather morbid and even inappropriate. My answer is that what is *genuinely* inappropriate is instantly discarded by the ethical and intuitive artist. I have great sympathy for *seemingly* inappropriate things, because they are the very stuff of a child's life, usually stifled by that child, never aired and clarified, and in the end causing an enormous grief and suffering to that child, and worse, occasionally handicapping the adult that that child becomes. Our job as artist needs to be to air those odd and misguided moments of childhood and show them as typical, even normal, occasionally exorcisable. Now, a pertinent theme in *Outside Over There* has to do with the fear of loss, the child's fear of being separated from beloved parents or siblings. That theme relates precisely to my terror as a child — exactly the terror I experienced in March 1932 when I was nearly four years old, and Charles Lindbergh's baby was kidnapped.

There may be a few of you here old enough to recollect that moment, but I recollect the headlines, I recollect the weather; I cannot go through a single March, and I haven't since then, without stopping and saying, this is March the first. I can only thank heaven that there was no television to explore, more graphically and hysterically than did the daily papers back then, the terrible days that followed. (How do children today survive watching the Lebanon massacre, when on the seven o'clock, eight o'clock, ten o'clock news you can see the corpses being devoured by flies?) I remember just headlines, photographs that were penetrating and indelible — I don't know that any of us know what children do with such images. I hope they all become artists and solve it that way. Suffice it to say, I was aware of everything related to the kidnapping case, and although it was never directly mentioned to me, I *knew* my parents were fearful for me. It took my colossally tedious and much disliked uncle to suggest that kidnappers had no interest in poor immigrant kids. It would have shocked me to know the kidnappers would have rejected me. My father obviously felt the same, for I remember that despite the Depression, he had new, very tight screens put into our bedrooms, and I remember sleeping, a stick on the floor, my brother and I in one bed, and my sister in another. So we regarded ourselves very highly. Surely, we were good material for kidnappers.

I can laugh at it now; it was no laughing matter then. There was no one to help me with the terror, no one to discuss it with, no one to make sense out of it. It became, thus, completely *my* terror. I absorbed, as children will, the external terror, and then fatefully internalized it, lived with it, dreamed of it, had nightmares involving poor Charlie Lindbergh's baby over and over for years — I never told my parents about that. And I only came to exorcise it, sort of, very sort of, nearly forty-five years later when I wrote *Outside Over There*. I make it sound easier and more satisfying than it was. Only in the movies are there totally successful exorcisms.

Now, in thinking of the Lindbergh case, two things collide in me that may sound oddly personal, but they are of extraordinary interest to me, and because I have already used them in a book, I have sufficiently objectified them. I was nearly four and had just gotten over what was very typical of the thirties kids — we had endless diseases. Occasionally, kids died from them, because there were not many vaccines or shots, so we all got measles, mumps, and whooping cough and the rest. Now I got them bad, apparently, all from my beloved elder sister, it turns out. When I was about three, three-and-a-half, I got scarlet fever compounded by pneumonia, and did nearly die. I do have a recollection of that period, of coming out of it, convalescing, and of my mother's almost insane hysteria concerning me. God knows what she had been through. It was very shortly after that, that the Lindbergh case occurred.

What do children make of death, of almost dying? My parents were not subtle or educated people. If I was nearly dying, they shouted it to the rooftops, *He is nearly dying.* It was shouted within my hearing; everyone came to mourn me long before I went. My father did something which was customary in his village; he dressed me in white garments so that I would be mistaken for an angel, and I would be taken. It was perfectly clear to me that nobody expected to have me around for very long, and yet, again, it was never a discussable issue. I couldn't even turn to my mother and my father and say, "Will I die?" I just knew I could go anytime.

Suddenly, this was all crystalized, traumatized, by the then most famous baby in the entire world, which was Charles Lindbergh, Jr. The most important man — if you put together Kennedy and John Travolta and any number of superstars, you have what we then thought of as Colonel Lindbergh. He was married to the most beautiful young woman in the world, the daughter of the Mexican ambassador, a poetess. She flew airplanes while she was pregnant; she did the most extraordinary things. They had this fabulous house in Hopewell, New Jersey; you saw pictures of it every day. Every bit of her pregnancy was reported, as in the case of the Dionne quintuplets a few years later.

The baby is born; it is the perfect baby. It is blond and curly-haired and blue-eyed, and you see its picture every day: what it ate, what it didn't eat, how it dressed, how it didn't dress, and when it was just over a year old, it was snatched, as we now say. Well, surely I can't recover those days of my childhood except to piece them together logically. It seems to me that if I felt vulnerable as a child, that I could die, in my house, with my father and mother hovering over me, and if Charlie Lindbergh — who was much more secure than I was, much better-looking, had a much better life, with German shepherds, nannies, servants, pilots, airplanes there in the house, whatever you want — could be taken at something like eight in the evening, which was how it happened, with his parents sitting down in the library, on a reasonably mild evening in early March, with dogs and nurses watching all through the house — this must have absolutely terrified me, that as children, we were so absolutely vulnerable, and that, in fact, a Lindbergh baby could be taken away. He was found two months later, dead, in a wood that was gruesomely covered by the daily news and the tabloids. I think what happened to me was a conjunction of anxieties, that I too could surely die. If he could, I could.

The most important thing for me in *Outside Over There* was for Ida to recover her baby. The change was once and for all to bring Charlie back alive. It didn't happen in real life — alas, it couldn't happen in real life — but in fiction, and to give myself pleasure, and to give the child self in me justice, I recovered the baby that was not recovered in 1932, and I gave the job to my sister, who was very disgruntled about it when she read it. But it also recovered the entire moment of love I felt for my sister and her love for me, which was mixed with passionate hatred, with demonic forces. I must have sensed that as a child, and I must have somehow acquiesced to it or resigned myself to it. Being in the hands of a monstrous adult (she could have been my mother, and most of the time I thought she was; I saw more of her than I saw of my mother, and I actually came to appreciate that later) creates a duality that every child has to live with, when the person in charge turns from demon to lover. The sister-in-charge can be as cold as ice; the sister can be warm and passionate; the sister hovers over you and dresses you. I think this typical of child life; it is also strangely unreported in works of art about children.

Some people say, "Why are you so serious about this? Children's books are supposed to be happy, playful things," and I say, "Nonsense." I mean, surely, they could be, and there are many children's books that are. Nobody wants to make children miserable, but I fear they are so shrewd, they know exactly what will frighten their parents, they know what not to ask. They can't move out, they'll have to wait another seventeen years before they get their first apartment, so they have to figure out the lay of the land. What do you say to Mama and Papa that doesn't upset Mama and Papa? So they learn to talk to Mama and Papa, and then they learn to talk to themselves, and then they learn to talk to each other. It's a whole different language and a whole different world upstairs. Of course, I'm generalizing. There must be enlightened parents who talk to their children; they are very few and far between, I suspect — but *Outside Over There* was an attempt to come to grips, at age fifty, with something which I had not come to grips with from the age of three on: how to support the knowledge of my own demise. Now, this is a question that children ask all the time. When I was much older — during the war, when everybody was dying all over the place — I was bold enough to ask my father if he would die. He lied and said that he promised he never would. It was perfectly logical; of course he would say that. I was obviously in a state of great upset when I asked the question. He shouldn't have lied, however, because some years later, when I was forty-three and my father was dying and I was with him — one of those events I treasure — the very first thing that came to my head, and I never remembered it until the moment of his death, was that he promised he wouldn't do it.

A book is an act of devotion, a passionate search for grace, a great joy of creation, and perhaps, to some degree, an exorcism of childhood nightmares and confusion. But that is only a small part of the creative process. It is a major act of faith that says we can, through knowledge, experience, and art, help the child who still lives in us to understand an old wrong and begin to be healed, to enjoy what is the natural right of all children, to be happy and to thrive. I'm frequently asked, especially by children, where the "Wild Things" came from. In truth, I do not know. But I make up answers to amuse children and, occasionally, adults, and perhaps those answers are closer to the truth than I would like to admit. After all, *I* make them up, and as Freud said, "It's your dream, honey."

I started with a title called "Where the Wild Horses Are." I loved that title. I had it for about two years. It sounded so poetic. There was only one *big* problem, which was that I couldn't draw horses, and if they were going to be the main image of a book that I was doing. . . . So I tried any number of things that I *could* draw. Now, it will tell you everything when I say that I came down to "things" to make it as general as possible and as easy for myself as possible. At first, there were typical, banal creatures, winged monstrosities. I tried to stay away from the creatures that I really loved, such as King Kong or movie creatures that I had grown up on. I thought that was certainly not classy enough for children's books, not classy enough for my first picture book, and this was my first picture book.

Then they began to come; they just began to appear on paper. Their source, or what they were, where they came from, was never clear to me, never questioned. When I had them, I knew they were right, and then they had names, had personalities, and it became no problem after that. But then the children became so curious, and the children would recognize different people *in* them, and their letters were full of, "Do you know my Aunt Martha?" or worse, "Do you know my mother?" So finally, I concocted an answer, and my answer is this: that the "Wild Things" are Jewish relatives, and that is as close as I can recollect, and it comes to Sundays in Brooklyn, Sundays of my mother cooking meals for relatives.

I was a very ungenerous child; I hated sharing our food with relatives. I didn't like my relatives at all. They were uncles and aunts on my mother's side, relatives who were brought over before the war, and it seemed to me they just hung around all the time; slept over too long, ate too much, and yakked too much. And then the Sundays would come, the intolerable Sundays, when my sister and my brother and I were well dressed; we didn't go out, and we sat, and my mother was a terribly slow cooker. She took forever, and *they* would be in the living room. They would be just innocent adults, although I hated them passionately. They didn't know how to talk to us; we were not allowed to go to our room; we *had* to sit with them.

When the relatives sat and stared at you, you were aware of the most gruesome things, such as moles on noses and extra-long hairs coming out of noses. You'd concentrate on anything but what they were saying. And then their faces drew closer, and you saw the bloodshot eyes, and you saw the very bad teeth. You know how we all hold our breath when we are with children in the train or subway, and some poor helpless person comes in who is lame or handicapped, you pray your child will not open his or her mouth. Usually, he or she does. We didn't dare.

Now, these people were looming over us, food odors coming from the kitchen taking forever to come to a head, them getting hungrier and hungrier, leaning over and doing what they think are endearing things like teasing your cheek and pinching the flesh so that it left purple marks, and you're supposed to enjoy that. Saying things like, "You look so good we could eat you up," and your knowing that soon they will if she didn't hurry up in the kitchen. They were dreadful days, and they were looked forward to with great trembling. So that, in fact, could be what the "Wild Things" are — the great revenge on my mother and my father and my uncles and my aunts. It's curious, because children always refer to them as *their* parents and relatives, as though I had drawn very specific members of *their* family. There's no humor in these letters. That's what's so marvelous about them; they're deadly serious.

Let me tell you another anecdote that relates to my favorite invention. Rosie, who, by chance, is the only *real* child whose portrait I drew both literally and figuratively. She is a perfect example of life and art hilariously colliding. Rosie was an actual child who lived in Brooklyn in the forties. She was maybe eight or nine; I was about sixteen, just before I left home; it was toward the end of the war. I was very lonely — both my brother and brother-in-law were in the army; I had no friends on that particular street, and my great pleasure was to sit at the window and draw Rosie. I have no idea why I did it. We lived in a two-family house; we were on the top floor, and you could look right down, and she would come out every day, all dressed up like the whore of Babylon, her mother's garments, hats, pearls, dripping jewelry, all Fellini-esque.

You could see her ordering the day, sitting on the stoop, looking for victims. These streets were small streets; you couldn't cross a street, because you would get killed — we all knew that. You had to look up at the window for your parents to cross you. If they were not there to cross you, you couldn't cross. If you began to cross when they were not there, they appeared, magically, and screamed so that you probably would die of shock, just hearing the voice on the street. So Rosie had no opportunity but to make do with what she had, which was a small street of rather boring children, and I would watch her be Fellini. Sometimes she failed, sometimes she was immensely successful, but she'd sit there and plot, like a great black widow spider, and then the kids would come around because, although they resented the immense power she had over them, there was no one else to turn to. She'd seen the movies, she'd listened to the radio — there was no television at that point, or very few people had television sets — so they depended entirely on her for feedback.

Typical of Rosie's stories, when she was having trouble holding the kids' attention, is a line I actually used in a play I did about Rosie. When all things were bad, and she couldn't rouse the kids, and very often they would become truculent and say, "To hell with you, Rosie" or sit in a corner and be cruel to her, she would give a very fateful line that always worked; it worked with me, too, just watching her. She would say, "Did you hear who died?" Well . . . fantastic line. You knew she was going to lie, but it just made no difference, because it was the way she said it. Her timing was perfection, her coolness, her aloofness — every head would turn, and we were all sucked in, and there was I, dizzy with pencil, writing out whatever she was about to say.

She did this on a number of occasions, but my favorite "Did you hear who died?" day was about her grandmother; she said her grandmother died, and then, of course, came a great chorus of "Oh, she did not; you're crazy." She let that pass; she never picked fights, she would just wait for them to stop, and then she said, "She died. She died early in the dawn." She was very dramatic. Her room was right under her grandmother's — their house was directly opposite mine, so I could see this typical Sicilian family. Grandma was always beating rugs and mattresses and linens — she must have had a lot of aggression. All mothers and grandmothers did that, but I don't think those straw-matted instruments exist anymore. Well, it seems that one dawn, Grandma got up — I guess just so turned on she couldn't resist — and began to beat a mattress in the window. She did this with such vim and vigor, that she lost her breath. She choked, and she fell down on to the floor. Rosie heard the thud; no one else did. She ran up to the attic room, and there was her grandmother struggling for breath, deep purple. She leaped onto the prone body and gave her grandmother the kiss of life.

The kids all said, "What? The kiss of life?" That was a big number then. Rosie gave it to her grandmother any number of times. (At this point, Rosie hurled down one of her friends on the stoop and gave her the kiss of life to show them what it was like.) The kiss of life failed. It failed. And to avoid upsetting her mother and father, she didn't tell them; she just called the mortuary. Apparently, her parents never found out that their mother died. And Rosie's grandmother was put in a kind of shopping bag, as Rosie described it, and taken away.

The story was fantastic. I stopped writing in the middle of it, because it was so vivid. At that moment — and I know this is true because I saw it — her grandmother came down the street with two enormous shopping bags, two great big puffy slippers on her feet. She was a ferocious, scowling woman who spoke no English. I don't know if she liked anyone or not, because I never understood her, but as she came to the stoop, there was Rosie with her friends seated right in the middle. Her grandmother said some tough, guttural thing, and, like the Red Sea, the kids just parted; they didn't fight her for a second. She went stomping up the stoop and she slammed the front door and she went stomping upstairs to the attic, and the kids closed in and they said, "Tell us again, Rosie."

She was the quintessential artist; she had turned everybody on. And she worked so hard; she did this every single day. Well, my interest in Rosie covered about a year and a half — in fact, up to the time when a dramatic moment occurred for both of us. It was the end of her reign; I'm glad I didn't see all of it. She was not the eldest, but as I say, the strongest and the most imaginative, but then she had some bad luck. A young girl moved in on the street who happened to be related to Rosie. Her name was Helen. Helen was about two years older. Rosie was a very plain child; Helen was a very pretty child. Helen immediately dominated the scene, took over. She was a wimp, she had no imagination, but she was aggressive, and she took Rosie's role away from her.

Rosie had never acknowledged my existence; she could easily have seen me — I was just up there all the time. She never looked. She would dress on the street, put on her long gloves, look in her looking glass. She did all of this in front of me without ever seeing me, or apparently seeing me. But Helen was that kind of blunt child who would see and say, and she looked up at me and she said, "What's he looking at?" with that intense look that some children have that makes you wither, because then I felt like some pervert. Rosie never looked up. She was smoothing her costume, or something, and she said, "That is Johnson, and he is taking down my life." She gave me a name and the correct occupation.

That was about 1945, I think; just about then, I left Brooklyn, finally, and made the grand escape to New York, crossed the Brooklyn Bridge, my mother weeping buckets because I was being lost to Sodom and Gomorrah and God knows what else, and I never saw Rosie again. In 1957, I did *A Sign on Rosie's Door,* which was a book based on experiences in the notes I'd taken about her, and we did a television show and an off-Broadway show.

Now we come to the moment when art and life collide hysterically, because at this point, finally, I had really convinced myself that I had invented Rosie. I had shown people my notebooks, I had shown my sketches, I had even done a very bad oil painting of Rosie from the window which I gave to my brother as a gift, but I didn't really quite believe her anymore. Anyway, there is a dreadful television program called 20/20 in New York. It's an interview program, and they called to ask if I would be interviewed for the show. I said yes, because I had just done *Outside Over There,* and the publisher at Harper was saying, "Do all you can; it's an odd book, Maurice." So I signed to do 20/20, and a very nice woman came and we chatted about what it would be, and her ideas were decent but banal — it was television — and one of the ideas was that we would go down memory lane. We would go back to Brooklyn and see what it was like to be back on those streets again.

I was curious to do it, although I winced a little at the conception of what might happen with this project, but we did go back. My family had moved endlessly in Brooklyn; my mother had an aversion to fresh paint, and in those faraway days, when you signed a contract for an apartment, it was freshly painted every third year by the landlord. Sounds incredible now. To avoid that fresh-paint smell, we packed and moved to a place that was a little older, so I saw all of Brooklyn, and probably every public school within a radius of about five miles. In choosing where to go back for this television show, I picked the only three places where I'd really been happy, and they were all within a radius of a few blocks.

I have to go into some detail to tell you this story. The cast of characters includes the lady running the 20/20 show, and there was Bob Brown, who was the interviewer. Now, Bob Brown is sort of your Marlboro-country type;

he towered over me. I have gotten over being short, after many years of analysis. When I talked to Dick Cavett, I was happy as a clam, because he was half my size, but in having to deal with Bob Brown, there was another whole problem, because he was very tall, very courtly, with a rich baritone — I disliked him, in other words. So there's the lady, there's Bob, who was really a very nice man, and then there's John. John, who's a very turned-off guy, himself came from Brooklyn, never heard of me, cannot imagine why they're making a fuss over this person; they just did Elizabeth Taylor or somebody really famous, and who is this man who does kiddie books? It was written all over him, but he was, nevertheless, the cameraman.

We go back to the street.

Now, you see all these people. You go to the first house that I lived in, on West Sixth Street off King's Highway. It's a regular day in the week, with very fat ladies with their hair in curlers, as there have always been on West Sixth Street off King's Highway, and there I am, seated on a stoop with my raincoat, having a serious discussion with Bob Brown towering over me, John taking the film, chewing gum and looking very bored, I'm talking about my life in Brooklyn, and people gathering and all saying, "Isn't that Bob Brown from 20/20?" Very vexing, because no one knew who I was, and they'd all come over and say to Brown, "Who is that little man you're talking to?" It was hard going for a while.

We went to another street, where the same thing occurred, and then we went to the third street, which was Rosie's. I had not been there since I had left. I walked to the very place we had lived, I looked across the street, and there was her house. Nothing, nothing had changed; nothing changes in Brooklyn, ever. A crowd gathered. I could see people in her house; they all looked Italian, they all looked like her. My heart was beating: could she be around? They were all saying the same thing: "Is that Bob Brown from 20/20?"

We go through the thing: Would I like to knock? Would the real Rosie please stand up? I said flatly: No, I wouldn't tolerate that, invading her privacy, and so on. However, once I was there, it was irresistible. The camera had stopped, the interview was over, they were not going to film it, and at that point I said, "Excuse me, I have to find out." Meanwhile, the cameraman, John — you remember him — is listening to this endless babble about this little girl. I mean, why is a grown man carrying on about a little girl? I cross the street, I tap on the door, it bursts open, and women come flocking to the door, and they all say at once, "Is that Bob Brown from 20/20?"

I said, "Yes, can I ask you a question? Is it possible that you know if a girl ever lived here named Rosie?" And a woman said, "Sure, my cousin." I nearly fainted. I said, "Rosie, Really Rosie?" Well, she never heard of Really Rosie, but she invited us in. The whole crew came in. She was intrigued; what did I know about her cousin Rose? We sat down. I said, "You have no idea." So I told her who I was. She knew nothing, she was embarrassed, she never reads children's books, her children never read children's books. Was Rose still alive? Well, of course Rose was still alive; Rose was now forty-two. Was she well? Yes, she was well, and this woman was stunned that Rose could have been my muse.

At a certain point I said, "There's one thing that really puzzles me, that all these years I've called her Rosie, I could not remember her last name. It was one of those difficult Sicilian names that you almost remember, but don't quite. What was her last name?" She said it *was* really a tough name; her last name was Stacompiano. I said, of course, I knew as soon as I heard it, Rosie Stacompiano. At that moment, there was a crash. We turned, and there was John, looking like he's had a seizure, the very first time he's looked interested at all in any of these events. His eyes are moving in circles; I've never seen anything like it. The woman who invited us in is now looking less cordial. "What's wrong with him?" she said very sharply.

"I don't know what's wrong with him — John, what's wrong with you?" He staggered into the middle of this little group that's seated around on couches and chairs, and then — as in Verdi or, better, Gilbert and Sullivan — he said, "Did you say . . . Rosie Stacompiano?" And we, as in Gilbert and Sullivan, we all said in chorus, "Yes, Rosie Stacompiano." He flattened out, he really did; he fell into a chair. He'd been hearing about this little girl and me for all these days, and when he could finally speak, he said, "She was my sweetheart."

It turned out he was engaged to my Rosie. So not only was Rosie becoming intensely real — more than I rather wished, as a matter of fact — but here was the man she'd been engaged to. He called up his mother — of course, she lived only seven blocks away, *everybody* only lives seven blocks away from everybody else in Brooklyn — and shouted at his mother, as boys in Brooklyn do, to find his yearbook. His mother said she didn't have his yearbook, because she gave it to him when he got married, so he called up his wife, who also lived seven blocks away, to find the yearbook. She found the yearbook, she rushed over; I was dying to see what Rosie looked like. And there, in fact, was the yearbook, and there was the graduating class. Then I read: "Rosie Stacompiano: Prettiest Girl in Class, but Camera-Shy." She had not come for the graduation picture.

To make a long story short — not too short, at this point — the very mythical Rosie had become the very real Rosie, and now I had a new friend who was named John, who left messages on my phone machine all the time: "Hey, Maurice, how are you, guy? Rosie and I had dinner. She's fantastic."

I have not met Rosie. I finally called her — I got up the courage to call her. She was wonderfully sweet on the phone; she was profusely embarrassed and she said, "I have never heard of you, Mr. Sendak. I am so sorry, but one of my children knew a book you did about wild creatures, and so we know you're well known, through at least one book." And she wanted to know all about me; she had no recollection of me living across the street; she was stunned that I knew the names of all her friends, and her pet names for her friends. I also knew the names her friends had for her, which were not pet names. I knew about the great vindictive fights between herself and Helen. She had not a shred of memory about her childhood. The only thing she reacted to was when I sent her a care package of all the Rosie things. Her children were flabbergasted that anyone could have cared for their mother at all, and could have been turned on by this woman. She sent me a photograph of herself; she's an extremely beautiful woman. She said the oddest thing happened when she read *The Sign on Rosie's Door*, because I mentioned her make-believe name in that, Alinda; in the street she called herself Alinda. She knew no one had ever known she called herself Alinda in the street. She said, "It's so silly to become emotional about a children's book, but I really can't read *The Sign on Rosie's Door,* because when I come to the part where she's in the backyard, I begin to cry. I feel so foolish about crying when I read a children's book."

I said, "Well, what do you think upsets you?" and she said, "I don't know; I suppose it's because I wanted to do what I imagined, when I grew up, and I never did. I got married when I was eighteen, just out of school, and now I've got five children, and we work very hard, and I'd forgotten all about Alinda, and all about Pudgy (her best friend) and Dolly, and all the rest." Rather than giving her pleasure, it made her sad. But I have not met her. We almost had Thanksgiving, Christmas, New Year's together, and finally, obviously, we both wanted to and couldn't. Then her husband George called and said that it was best we didn't; that it was so upsetting to her, and so exciting to her, and so unreal, that we should leave it alone. We never met.

I'm going to end now by talking about my other kids, because my children are getting long in the tooth at this point. I often wondered, if they were real, what would become of them. Max surely is a child psychologist, at best; a TV soap-opera writer, at worst. Mickey is a hopeless but happy sensualist, living in Las Vegas, with a water bed in every room. Pierre's irrational and wrong-headed behavior clearly prepared him for a successful career in politics; I wish him well. Ida and the baby are still growing up. I, too — I hope — am still growing up.

Introduction to Lloyd Alexander

GREAT CHILDREN'S BOOKS come when writers capture the dreams of childhood with their skills grown wise. Every child dreams of heroic ventures. Lloyd Alexander has captured those dreams with the wiles of wit, invention, timing, and characters who become each reader's close friends or arch enemies. The style of his twenty-two books for young people is so quotable that perhaps the best introduction might be simply bits and pieces of his own fiction and commentary. Even a glimpse of his personal life and loves could be spiced up considerably by lines from his letters, autobiographical statements, and, amazingly, music-program notes. For this is not merely an accomplished writer we gather to hear tonight, but a promising violinist. Alas, the two careers have suffered an inverse ratio. Like his character Flewder Flamm in the Prydain Chronicles, Lloyd Alexander has had a string break for every tale stretched. And the elaboration of his wild and wonderful stories has wreaked havoc with his poor instrument. I read to you briefly from a recent concert program in which Lloyd played first — and only — violin. "Felix Mendelssohn's work," he writes, "is filled with a longing for faraway places. Listeners may experience a similar yearning."

On his early years Lloyd waxes eloquent. "The happiest thing about my childhood was: It ended." Of his insatiable reading in a family of nonreaders, he remembers especially "Ridpath's *History of the World* in three volumes — mainly volume one, with its magnificently lascivious engravings of Egyptian, Greek, and Roman women delightfully undraped. Ridpath taught me," maintains Alexander, "the joy of prurience and very likely accounted for my enduring love of classical antiquity." Also noted as important to his early development are copies of *Piggly Wiggily;* a venerable how-to book called *Personal Magnetism;* and — now to the heart of it — *King Arthur and His Knights.*

To pass succinctly by his self-education, his years abroad as a United States intelligence officer, and marriage in France to the subject of his book *Janine Is French,* his translations of Paul Éluard and Jean-Paul Sartre, and his other adult books during the 1950s and 1960s, let us get right to the discovery of Lloyd's place at the Round Table — a place earned, title by title, as valiantly as any seat in Camelot. Among many other honors, Lloyd won, in 1969, the Newbery Medal for *The High King,* last of his five books of the Prydain Chronicles; in 1971, the National Book Award for *The Marvelous Misadventures of Sebastian;* in 1982, the American Book Award for *Westmark,* first of three volumes in a remarkable series including *The Kestrel* and *The Beggar Queen.* Where a list might become tedious, a sampling substantiates the critics' kudos. All cite his characters, delineated with a pen stroke and developed with finesse. Meet Cabbarus, villain of *Westmark:* "As chief minister, he was entitled to sumptuous chambers in the new Juliana. He declined them. He kept his same quarters, setting an example of frugality and modesty; righteousness being always more believable when combined with dreariness." (p. 31)

Lloyd Alexander's villains are often the more powerful for being lost heroes, distorted by fatal flaws we all share. And his fantasy heroes are convincingly human — guileless, vulnerable, faulty, sometimes silly. The aforementioned Flewder Flamm, while brave beyond question, exaggerates his own bravery: "I can't help, ah, adding a little color to the facts," he sighs as another harp string breaks with another stretch of the truth. "Most facts need it so badly." (*Black Cauldron*, p. 21) The hero of *Westmark* is introduced with characteristic irony: "As for Theo, he loved virtue, despised injustice, and was always slightly hungry." (p. 4) In fact, Lloyd Alexander dedicates *The Kestrel* to "Those who know that they are only human but who try not to be any less." His plots are remarkable both for complexity and pace, two elements not always compatible in literature. Even his descriptions lend either suspense or comic relief, as this passage from *Westmark* attests:

> The lodging house at the end of Strawmarket Street stood as one of the marvels of Freyborg: the marvel being that it stood at all. The spiderwebs in every corner appeared to be its strongest support. The narrow staircase lurched up three flights and stayed in place out of habit. Mold flowered from cracks in the walls. The roof shed its tiles like autumn leaves. The lodgings, nevertheless, had two things to recommend them: cheap rent and a landlord who never asked questions.[1]

His fantasy is realistic, his realism fantastic. As one *Booklist* reviewer confided: "I know he's contriving this plot, but I'm so anxious to find out what happens I don't even care. . . . He's got me right where he wants me." His themes are dramatically realized, his treatment of conflicts between good and evil, subtle.

It is fitting that Lloyd writes in one of his acceptance speeches: "I rejoice in our frailties as much as in our virtues. Our virtues tend to come and go, depending on our circumstances. Our frailties stay faithfully with us. We can count on them. They validate our humanity and keep us from being too pleased with ourselves."

This from a person who often initiates correspondence and always answers it, who is both humble about his own work and generous about others'. His remarks on writing as dissimilar from his own as Virginia Hamilton's were memorable for their sympathetic insight when he was an NBA judge speaking on her behalf. After growing to love an author through his books, one is sometimes unpleasantly surprised to meet a very different person in the flesh. But in the case of Lloyd Alexander, the man lives up to the writer. May I present Lloyd Alexander.

Lloyd Alexander
Grand Illusions
May 4, 1984

SOMEHOW, WHEN I was about ten years old, I managed to get my hands on a book of Greek mythology. I discovered the Olympian gods and goddesses. They fascinated me. I was completely caught up by those marvelous deities and thoroughly believed in their existence. I also believed, with equal fervor, in Santa Claus, the apostles' creed, King Arthur, and the magical power of wishbones. I saw no reason why one should exclude another. Sir Galahad chasing the Holy Grail, St. Patrick chasing the snakes, and St. George chasing the dragon all shared my devotion.

I happily added Zeus, Athene, foam-born Aphrodite, and their colleagues to my private pantheon. I wanted to know more about them. One evening, I brought up the subject with a family friend, a stout, pear-shaped man, a frequent visitor named Mr. Rockwell. Years before, he had been an episcopal clergyman. I never learned exactly why he left the church; it was something vague that involved a parishioner's wife.

More to my interest, Mr. Rockwell had traveled considerably and had actually been to Greece. I asked if he had gone to Mount Olympus and if he had seen traces of the inhabitants. Not that I expected the Immortals to reveal themselves to followers of a Cook's tour; but there might have been relics. Even if the Olympians had changed neighborhoods after so many centuries, they should have left something behind. After all, when my family moved into a different house, we constantly found small reminders of the previous occupants.

Mr. Rockwell, to my dismay, had found nothing. Worse, he went on to tell me that none of those Immortals existed; not now, not then, not ever. He assured me they were only stories, no more than fairy tales, with no reality whatever.

I refused to believe that. They must have existed. The Greeks, who were certainly no fools, believed they did. Here was my book, describing them in detail. There were even illustrations. In color. I protested, almost in tears, insisted, argued, pleaded for them to be true.

My parents listened to our discussion with consternation and horror. Talking back to an adult was bad enough; but now they began to fear they had raised some kind of pagan. To my family, pagan was only one degree worse than Presbyterian.

Finally, Mr. Rockwell ended our colloquy with the adult's unanswerable, oracular pronouncement: "You'll understand when you're older."

Yes. Well, with patience and determination I did eventually grow older. I won't swear that I really understood.

Growing up surely must be more than just a process of demythologizing. As a matter of practicality and survival, we do have to learn the difference between the real and the imaginary. In day-to-day matters, we don't want to mix them up. I wouldn't, for example, feel comfortable in an airplane if the pilot decided to hand over the controls to the Easter Bunny.

But I wonder, in another sense, if what we call the reality principle may be only a means of helping us agree on what is possible and what isn't. This can be harder than it seems. These days, if we succeed in believing six impossible things before breakfast, we'll only be given six more at dinner, along with the evening news. Yesterday's impossibility becomes today's reality, and sometimes tomorrow's boredom. Like, what else is new? Achievements in technology don't boggle the imagination quite as much as they once did. We've even been able to live with the impossible idea that some idiot somewhere can turn us all into radioactive landfill.

But what about other impossibilities?

Child-soldiers clearing mine fields with their own bodies? Thousands of people vanished, disappeared, as if by a monstrous conjuring trick? Assassins boasting of their work? Poets locked in madhouses or labor camps? Impossible? No. And the worst of it is: None of this is essentially new. Only the hardware has improved. The impossible becomes the possible. The possible becomes the unspeakable.

We can justifiably raise the question: Is the world mad — or just the people in it? If we can make no sense of it, what sense can a child make? Perhaps a child might understand it better, viewing it as merely typical adult irrationality.

The temptation is strong to see it all as hallucination. Small wonder that Shakespeare concluded: "We are such stuff as dreams are made on. . . ." Or nightmares.

Mark Twain agreed with Shakespeare. In what must be one of the most bitterly humorous and most devastating novels — *The Mysterious Stranger* — Mark Twain gives this final speech to his angelic visitor (I'm quoting from the Harper 1916 edition, not the travesty aired a while ago on television):

> Strange indeed, [the angel tells the narrator] that you should not have suspected that your universe and its contents were only dreams, visions, fiction! Strange, because they are so frankly and hysterically insane. . . . These things are all impossible except in a dream . . . and you the maker of it. The dreammarks are all present; you should have recognized them earlier. Nothing exists but you. And you are but a thought . . . vagrant . . . homeless . . . wandering among empty eternities.

It is one of the bleakest visions in all fiction.

Lewis Mumford takes a somewhat different and more hopeful attitude:

> In the light of human consciousness, it is not man but the whole universe . . . that turns out to be impotent and insignificant. [The] physical universe is unable to behold itself except through the eyes of man, unable to speak for itself, except through the human voice, unable to know itself, except through human intelligence. . . . In short, without man's cumulative capacity to give symbolic form to experience, to reflect upon it and re-fashion it and project it, the physical universe would be as empty of meaning as a handless clock: its ticking would tell nothing. The mindfulness of man makes the difference.[2]

For all practical purposes, we assume the world does exist. It is a very real place, as we know all too well. This does not preclude having our own vision of it. More to the point is whether this vision enriches life or impoverishes it.

Civilization has been defined as an agreement to ignore the abyss. I would rather call it an attempt to understand the abyss, as we have tried constantly to do by means of religion, philosophy, and art. In other words, by mental constructs; by thoughts, without a tangible physical existence of their own. For these intangible structures, I propose the term *illusion*.

I must, here, make a crucial distinction between illusion and delusion. Delusion is a belief held in spite of unquestionable evidence to the contrary. Delusion claims to know reality, but has barely a nodding acquaintance with it. Private delusions are not necessarily harmful. For example, I cherish the delusion that I can play the fiddle. This may annoy my neighbors, but causes no permanent damage. Delusion may be comic or tragic, sad or silly. It may even show an occasional flash of bizarre imagination: the perception of catsup as a vegetable.

Society demands reasonable limits to the unreasonable. People whose delusions overstep a certain boundary usually go for treatment in mental hospitals; in extreme cases, they go into politics. But we run into trouble when private delusion is offered as public truth. When we are told with all solemn assurance that the world is shatterproof; that it can be ravaged with impunity; that some people are less human than others; and some not really human at all. Delusion, ultimately, does not draw us toward life. It destroys more than it creates. It gives no vision, only blindness. It does not help us to understand the abyss — it becomes part of it.

Illusion, I suggest, is quite the opposite and serves an essential and valuable purpose. Illusion is what appears to be real, but in actuality, does not exist. Illusion *seems*. Yet, it can seem to be more real than reality. It only pretends to be true, but it can show facets of truth we never saw before. Illusion, in this sense, is an illumination. It reveals, it does not obscure. It takes us toward life, not away from it.

When it is persuasive, when it thoroughly convinces us, we call it art, the grandest of all illusions. Without substance, it nevertheless can make us laugh or cry, delight or terrify us. Without a life of its own, it creates a life for us; that is, it lets us create one for ourselves.

Though illusion deals with reality, it does not have to imitate it slavishly. Art is more than a game of surfaces. Others have made the point better than I can, so let me interrupt myself and read "Promenade de Picasso" by the French poet Jacques Prévert:

> On a perfectly round plate of real porcelain
> an apple poses
> for a painter of reality
> who tries vainly to paint
> the apple as it really is
> but the apple won't allow it
> the apple doesn't want its picture painted
> and so
> on its real plate
> quietly slyly
> without upsetting the applecart
> the apple disguises itself

as a beautiful piece of fruit
and the painter of reality
begins to realize
the apple's appearances are against him
and like a miserable pauper
like a poor soul who finds himself at the
> *mercy of a benevolent and charitable*
> *organization redoubtable in its*
> *benevolence charity and redoubtability*
the wretched painter of reality
suddenly finds himself unhappy prey
to an endless association of ideas
and the apple reminds him of
the Garden of Eden Adam and Eve
the serpent in the appletree
and original sin
and aboriginal art
and apple of discord
and William Tell
and when it's apple blossom time in Normandy
and even Isaac Newton
several times awarded first prize at the
> *Exposition of Universal Gravitation*
and the stunned painter loses sight of his model
and goes to sleep
And then Picasso
who was passing there as he passes everywhere
making himself at home
sees the apple the plate and the sleeping painter
Why paint an apple?
says Picasso
and Picasso eats the apple
and the apple says Thank you
and Picasso breaks the plate

and walks away smiling
and the painter torn from his dreams
like a tooth
finds himself alone before his unfinished canvas
and in the middle of his broken plate
the terrifying seeds of reality.[3]

Like painting, literature also tries to break through to the seeds of reality. So does that body of literature which speaks to the young: children's literature. A convenient term, but not expressive. To some, it implies a lesser form, not really serious, essentially second-rate. Well, yes, some children's books are second-rate. Some aren't good enough for children. But that number is relatively small, very small compared with the number of adult books not good enough for adults.

Regrettably — perhaps unavoidably, given the technicalities of publishing, cataloging, long-established habits, and so on — the term also implies an area shut off from adult literature. True, some books primarily speak to the young, just as some books primarily speak to adults; and some cross all age categories. Nevertheless, children's literature is not a hermetically sealed compartment. If it is perceived as such, we in the profession must take a certain amount of blame. Like all specialists, we tend — of necessity — to focus on our specialty. But we can, with every good intention, focus too closely on it. We can benefit from seeing children's literature in the context of literature in general.

By the same token, writers of adult novels would do well to study children's literature. For some years, the so-called "literary" novel has fallen into bad company. That is to say, it has fallen into the clutches of theoreticians: semiologists, structuralists, and all manner of literary philosophers — practically everybody but writers.

The "literary" novel has moved from the hands of the reader to the dissecting table of the anatomist. It has become not a work of art but a "text" — a pretext, I should say — for doctrinaires to expound their particular doctrines. What is written about the novel becomes more important than the novel itself, as if writers existed for the purpose of giving explicators something to explicate.

Writers have gone along with the trend, and even encouraged it. The Post-Modernists seemed to believe that a novel that told a comprehensible story, which included recognizably human characters or involved some discernible attitude toward the human condition, was outmoded. In its place, they substituted works written mainly to demonstrate one or another literary theory, the more abstruse the better. Actually, it was a marvelous idea, for the writers, if not the readers. It let authors become inscrutable. Readers who couldn't understand had only themselves to blame. It was a wonderful smoke screen, concealing an absolutely breathtaking scarcity of ideas. They built amazing labyrinths, elaborate mansions. There was only one trouble. The buildings were empty: nobody home.

I believe in every kind of experimentation, every technique that will stretch the limits of art for children as well as adults. The problem, it seems to me, lies not with techniques, not with old forms or new forms, but with the writers who use them. Forms are neither good nor bad in themselves. There are no bankrupt forms, only bankrupt talents.

In the adult novel, things are beginning to change. Umberto Eco, himself an academic and author of that unexpected best-seller *The Name of the Rose,* believes that narrative abstraction has reached a dead-end similar, he says, to what happened in painting:

> The avant-garde painters went on destroying the human image, and they arrived at abstract painting, then action painting, then the blank canvas. At one point it became impossible to go forward, and [they] had to rediscover the image. This is what writers have done who are coming back to plot.[4]

Commendable. But rather like the self-taught scientist who never read a textbook and spent years alone in his laboratory, finally emerging to announce a great discovery: that water was composed of two parts hydrogen and one part oxygen. Adult writers are rediscovering what children's writers always knew.

I can only repeat what I've said on other occasions: Children's literature is an area where art works as I believe it should work. That is, it delights, engages, illuminates. It involves its audience in ways that few modern adult novels do. The day is past when readers of Dickens crowded in front of his house demanding to know what was going to happen to Little Nell. Even our best modern adult novels no longer generate that same kind of excitement. But to a degree, this does happen with children's literature. Here, between writer and reader is a bond of affection: direct, personal, full of vitality.

I don't mean to wander away from my subject, the nature and value of illusion, because I must, finally, come to the key question: Can this illusion we call art offer anything useful and durable? For us, concerned with and for young people, the question is real and urgent. In the most literal sense, a matter of life and death. We have to ask: Can literature change our lives?

I believe so. It has been changing our lives ever since the invention of language. It was not the stone ax, not the tool, not the weapon that began to humanize us. It was language: language as tool, as weapon — and as magic spell. The process goes on. Says Lewis Mumford:

> Right up to our own time, language has surpassed any other form of tool or machine as a technical instrument . . . it is the most transportable and stor- able, the most easily diffusible, of all social artifacts. . . . Language is the great container of culture . . . and no matter how much the outer scene changes, through language man retains an inner scene where he is at home with his own mind.[5]

The word can change the world — to the extent that it can, and does, change individual perceptions and atti- tudes. There are books that have changed our lives. We may not even recall their titles; they may have been mas- terpieces or trash wallows, but they have gone into the shaping of our personalities.

And yet, throughout history, the greatest achievements of art, music, and literature, the most persuasive, compas- sionate human messages have been forgotten in the blink of an eye. We have thousands of years of evidence to dem- onstrate that our pride in culture and civilization may not be an illusion but a delusion; that we have learned nothing or forgotten everything from the best of our teachers. We have every reason to believe that human nature is essen- tially wicked and destructive.

And yet, I don't believe that.

The answer, I think, is that we are neither devils nor angels. Instead, we are simply very fragile beings. Civilization is very fragile. It must, therefore, be constantly tended, nurtured, strengthened, and renewed. Often, our best efforts fail. We'd be Pollyanna or Dr. Pangloss if we never felt discouraged, but we'd be even more foolish if we gave way to despair. Each new generation is a new possibility.

William Morris speaks of "the battle which men fight and lose, and the thing they fought for comes about in spite of their defeat, and when it comes, turns out not to be what they meant, and other men have to fight for what they meant under a different name." [6]

It is an endless process. There is no Utopia at the end of it, because there is no end of it. We, who value children and literature, are a part of it, but only temporarily. Adults, we have more yesterdays than tomorrows. The young count on us for whatever wisdom we can offer — and quite sensibly ignore most of it. But we count on the young to do what we were not wise enough to do.

We have no guarantee of success. The profession of art is a trapeze act without a net. So is teaching. So is librarianship. So is parenting. But we can't be afraid of risk. Without risk, we can't grow. Without risk, we can't help others to grow.

Our resources are very modest: a few daubs of color, a few combinations of sounds, a few words on a page. Illusions, all. But what marvelous illusions! If we can believe in them, they may even cease to be illusions and become miracles. That is, they may let us perform the greatest miracle: turning hope into reality.

Is this too optimistic? I hope not. Even if it is, illusion has value nevertheless: the value of simply giving pleasure. Though I've gone on at some length — too long, I'm afraid — forgive me if I claim the author's privilege of not only quoting other people but quoting myself.

In a story called "The True Enchanter," to win his beloved Angharad, young Geraint is required to demonstrate his magical powers. And so he begins:

> In common, quiet words he spoke of waters and woodlands, of sea and sky, of men and women, of childhood and old age; of the wonder and beauty of living things, all closely woven one with the other as threads on the same loom.
>
> As he spoke, he stretched out his open hands, and all in the court fell silent, marveling. For now, born of his simple gesture, appeared flights of doves, fluttering and circling around him. Flowers blossomed at each motion of his fingers. He raised his arms and above his head stars glittered in a sparkling cloud and a shower of lights was scattered through the Great Hall.

His colleagues, however, accuse him of being a hoaxer and mere juggler. Geraint frankly admits it. "Sorcery is not my birthright," he says.

> I have no inborn powers. What I showed, I fashioned by myself. The birds you saw? No doves, only bits of white parchment. The flowers? Dry grass and tinted leaves. The stars? A handful of bright pebbles.
>
> I only helped you imagine these things to be more than what they are. If this pleased you for a few moments, I could ask nothing better.[7]

I hope to have done likewise.

NOTES

1. Lloyd Alexander, *Westmark* (New York: Dutton, 1981), p. 83.
2. Lewis Mumford, *The Myth of the Machine* (New York: Harcourt, 1966), pp. 31, 35.
3. Jacques Prévert, "Promenade de Picasso," *Paroles* (Paris: Le Point du Jour, 1947).
4. Umberto Eco, "Mysteries Join the Mainstream," *The New York Times Book Review*, January 15, 1984.
5. Mumford, op. cit., p. 96.
6. William Morris, "A Dream of John Ball," *New York Review of Books*, November 22, 1979.
7. Lloyd Alexander, "The True Enchanter," *The Foundling* (New York: Holt, Rinehart, and Winston, 1973), pp. 41, 43.

Introduction to Katherine Paterson

WHEN I STARTED TO WORRY about this introduction one recent midnight, I thought I would just dip into passages from several of Katherine Paterson's books that I had read some time ago. About two o'clock in the morning, I was still sitting up in bed, tears streaming down my face onto the last pages of the first book I picked up, *A Bridge to Terabithia*. Leslie had just died, and like a fool, all I could do was snuffle into a huge wad of Kleenex. The moral is, don't try to skim a good novel. So I allowed a lot more time for *The Great Gilly Hopkins* the next night, and for *Jacob Have I Loved* the next, and so on.

What I discovered to be most astonishing about Paterson's array of work is her ability to build, with an absorbing intensity, totally different worlds of character and situation within a genre of realism which, in the hands of the majority of juvenile writers, becomes repetitive and banal. She has an emotional hotline into the deepest concerns of childhood — peopling, plotting, setting, and styling stories into the kind of simple, natural shapes that carry the most complex meanings: the death of a friend in *A Bridge to Terabithia;* the release of defenses against having never been loved in *The Great Gilly Hopkins;* the fierce quest for identity in *Jacob Have I Loved;* and, the acceptance of a great gift of talent in *Come Sing, Jimmy Jo.* Her canon of historical fiction, set in China, where she was born, and Japan, where she studied, has an emotional immediacy similar to that of her novels set in rural Appalachia or the Maryland coast.

They are all characterized by a moral toughness that leaves no room for the sweet or the didactic or even the easy way out. Jess will forever feel pain and guilt over Leslie's drowning, but there is redemption in bequeathing to his sister the imaginative legacy of his dead friend.

To the only person who has ever persisted past her obnoxious ways into her neglected heart, Gilly Hopkins says:

> "Dammit, Trotter. Don't try to make a stinking Christian out of me."
>
> "I wouldn't try to make nothing out of you." There was a quiet at the other end of the line. "Me and William Ernest and Mr. Randolph kinda like you the way you are."
>
> "Go to hell, Trotter," Gilly said softly.
>
> A sigh. "Well, I don't know about that. I had planned on settling permanently somewheres else."
>
> "Trotter" — She couldn't push the word hard enough to keep the squeak out — "I love you."
>
> "I know, baby. I love you, too." [1]

Paterson's other novels reveal equally hard-won resolutions. Throughout a stormy childhood and adolescence, Louise never comes to terms with her twin sister, only her adult observations finally bring a separate peace at the end of *Jacob Have I Loved.*

The Rebels of the Heavenly Kingdom strips patriotism

and idealism for a look at power, greed, and the real ends of war.

Jimmy Jo has to see beyond the weakness and betrayal in both his parents' actions, past the pathetic hysteria of his country-music fans, to where his own strength lies, in the mountains, in mountain music, and in the old mountain woman and her son, who have raised him in their own image.

A reviewer comes to expect a good many indifferent books, to enjoy chortling over the irretrievably bad ones, to anticipate with relish the reliable storytellers. But aside from those obvious categories is the rare privilege of discovering a first novel that develops into fullblown work marking the exceptional writer. One seldom comes along. Katherine Paterson came along while I was an editor at *Booklist,* and by clerical error, one of her first titles was included on the infamous "Considered but not reviewed" list. Following a humble correction note and a glowing review for *The Master Puppeteer* came an array of stars in our journal and most others for Paterson's later books, plus two Newbery Awards, for *A Bridge to Terabithia* in 1978 and *Jacob Have I Loved* in 1981, with a National Book Award for *The Great Gilly Hopkins* in 1977.

One can read all this in biographical dictionaries, along with the facts of Paterson's life, but none of it is as revealing as the truth of her work. Writer, characters, and readers seem to get peeled away layer by layer. There was a point at which I thought Paterson wrote too close to home for me to be objective. The rope those children use to swing over the gully into the land of Terabithia is a dead ringer for the one I used to swing out over a mountainside in Tennessee. But that rope seems to swing into just about everybody's private world. After *Terabithia* began to circulate, I overheard comments and conversations, one, among librarians who were saying, "Gee, I can't believe they gave the Newbery to a book the children are *reading*"; another, between two children, one of whom had led the other through close underbrush across a maze of logs and stones into a land she considered private and holy, christened Terabithia, where she had built a shelter from her own storms.

There are many bridges in Paterson's fiction, both real and symbolic. The strongest one stretches from a skilled and caring writer to readers who need all the skills and care they can get.

Katherine Paterson.

Katherine Paterson

Tell All the Truth
but Tell It Slant
May 3, 1985

AS YOU MUST REALIZE, titles are very important to a writer. When I choose a title for a book, it is a promise to myself of what I hope the story will fulfill. I choose each as carefully as we chose the names of our children. I had a book come out in April, a book that I loved writing. Usually, writing a book is like raising a child. There are many joys along the way, but it is not unmixed joy. Twice, however, I have written books that I really had fun writing, books during which the days of frustration and confusion were so few as to be quickly forgotten. This last book was just such a book. To me, *Please Welcome Jimmy Jo Johnson* was a warm and simple melody that I delighted to sing. My family loved it, my editor was pleased with it — that is, she liked everything but my title. Over a period of months, we struggled to find a title for what I had thought was an open, straightforward story. We must have tried and discarded thirty titles. I would lie awake at night thinking up titles. I remember one morning addressing the breakfast table with an inspiration. "How about this one?" I asked, trumpeting what I thought was a sure winner. Mary looked up over her glass of milk and said with characteristic compassion, "You're really desperate, aren't you, Mom?"

I first began worrying about the title of this lecture over a year ago. My feeling at that time was that I wanted to talk about story. I even played with a title taken from an old Sunday school hymn, "I Love to Tell the Story." Because I do. I do not like to write speeches, but I love to tell stories. Most people do. Telling stories is what makes us human.

During the 1984 presidential campaign, the Washington columnist Carl Rowan wrote about a visit President Reagan had made to an aging inner-city school building in the District of Columbia. The column read:

> At the Jefferson Junior High School here Monday, Mr. Reagan boasted that he "attended six elementary schools and one high school. And in none of them was there a library." He [the President] truly believes that he can sell voters the idea that facilities, libraries, books do not matter, which means he thinks he also can convince parents that his reductions in federal support do not matter — at least not where there is "humanity" inside dilapidated, ill-supplied school buildings.[2]

I realize that anything I say in response to this story will be cloaked in my own vested interest. When schools decide that libraries are frills, the Patersons are going to have a hard time paying the college bills. But I would like to think it is not simply my own vested interest that is at stake here. I believe that books, that novels, are vital to that humanity that the President says he wants us to value. We are the species that tell each other stories.

When I was in college, the common idea was that the dividing line between animal and human was the ability to make tools. We have these wonderful thumbs, you see, and it allows us to make tools, so we can sharpen rocks and pitch them at rabbits. Jane Goodall has shattered that theory. Chimpanzees make tools. We have to look further. What is our distinction? Is it the ability to communicate? No, I think it's more complicated than that. As the scientist Jacob Bronowski reminds us, animals can communicate with one another. They give signals of danger or mating calls. But they do not, as far as we know, name things. They do not, again, as far as we know, break down a cry into individual words and then arrange those words into new sentences with different meanings.[3] Even more basically, as Bronowski explains elsewhere, animals do not create images. Animals, you see, lack imagination, which seems to be a distinctly human gift. "The power," Bronowski says, "that man has over nature and himself, and that a dog lacks, lies in his command of imaginary experience. He alone has the symbols which fix the past and play with the future, possible and impossible."[4] We are the animals that tell each other stories, and that has made all the difference.

I was lecturing at a university two years ago and had the privilege (and I use the word a bit loosely here) of having lunch with a small group of graduate students who wanted to eat with and/or up the visiting writer. Now, one young man in the group was very proud to relate how he had gone from the foolish faith of his childhood to a wonderfully sophisticated nihilism, so he felt compelled to attack me on the grounds of what he regarded as my childish religiosity.

In the course of the discussion I said something about

the stories of the Bible, and he screeched in delighted triumph. "So," he yelled loud enough for the entire restaurant to hear. "So! You think they're merely stories."

"If you knew what I meant by *stories*," I answered, and I hope in a quiet, polite, intelligent, mature manner, "if you knew what I meant by *stories*, you would never use the word *mere* to describe them."

I guess my luncheon companion scared me off. I was afraid that if I used an old Sunday school hymn for the title of my lecture, I'd be inviting shrieks from any stray nihilist who might be in the audience, so I turned from the hymnal to Emily Dickinson for the text for this evening:

> *Tell all the Truth but tell it slant —*
> *Success in Circuit lies*
> *Too bright for our infirm Delight*
> *The Truth's superb surprise*
> *As Lightning to the Child eased*
> *With explanation kind*
> *The Truth must dazzle gradually*
> *Or every man be blind —* [5]

"And," as my grandmother used to say, "that goes for women, too."

Now, of course, there is no such thing as telling "all the truth." There is no such thing as knowing even a fraction of it. Dickinson knew that as well as the next poet. I think what we're talking about here is not knowing the truth so much as seeing it. Let me turn to another poet to help me explain the distinction.

In his foreword to *J.B.*, Archibald MacLeish describes Job's search for the meaning of his afflictions. "Job," MacLeish tells us "wants *justice* of the universe. He needs to know the reason for his wretchedness. And it is in those repeated cries of his that we hear most clearly our own voices. For our age is an age haunted and riven by the need to know. Not only is our science full of it, but our arts, also. And it is here, or so it seems to me, that our story and the story of Job come closest to each other. Job is not *answered* in the Bible by the voice out of the whirling wing. He is *silenced* by it — silenced by some thirty or forty of the greatest lines in all literature — silenced by the might and majesty and magnificence of the creation. He is brought, not to *know*, but to *see*."⁶

This is one reason I love stories. They allow us a vision of the unknowable. They let us perceive what we cannot prove. They let us see on a slant what we could never confront directly. Let us illustrate with a story.

Moses is in the wilderness, and, as usual, the people of Israel are, as the King James has it, "murmuring." *Murmuring* being a polite term for armed mutiny. Moses is at the point of despair. He needs a sign from God to keep him from going completely under. As Bishop Tutu observed recently: "There are those occasions when you say, 'Well, God, you are in charge. This is your world. But do you think you could make it slightly more obvious?' " (At Union Theological Seminary, New York City, on October 25, 1984.) Moses was at one of those occasions, and he wanted God to make his authority more than *slightly* obvious. "I beseech thee," Moses prays, "show me thy glory."

At this point I need to say something about the copy editor of the Book of Exodus. In chapter 33, the fellow must have nodded, because in verse 11, we read, "And the Lord spake unto Moses face to face, as a man speaketh unto his friend." But now, not ten verses later, God says to Moses, "Thou canst not see my face: for there shall no man see me and live." And then there follows the good part of the story, for the Lord goes on to say, "Behold, there is a place by me, and thou shalt stand upon a rock: And it shall come to pass, while my glory passeth by, that I will put thee in a cleft of the rock, and will cover thee with my hand while I pass by: And I will take away mine hand, and thou shalt see my back parts: but my face shall not be seen."

Isn't that a wonderful image? I'm grateful the copy editor didn't redline the contradiction. I can't picture Moses speaking face-to-face with God, but in that majestic covering and uncovering hand, we have protection and mercy and even humor, which may be inadvertent and the fault of the ancient translators, but still adds an irresistible charm to a story that we can tell and retell with awe and pleasure for another several thousand years.

"Too bright for our infirm Delight
The Truth's superb surprise . . ."

When it comes to Truth with a capital T, we will never "know" it in the scientific manner, but we might, if we are very fortunate or very blessed, peep through the cracks of the Almighty fingers and get a glimpse of the back parts.

I think that stories give us a way of peeping through those cracks. Now, people have always known this. The answer to the child's ubiquitous *why?* has been, from time immemorial, a story. As Kipling said, "No one in the world knew what truth was till someone had told a story."

But something peculiar has happened to us in the last generation or so. We seem to have reversed evolution. In our present thinking, it is the advanced person who sharpens rocks and the primitive one who tells stories.

Some of us in the field of children's books have been trying to speak out against the arms race. Whenever we do so, there is an earnest soul who feels obliged to challenge us. What right have we, whose lives are bound up in stories, to question those whose lives are devoted to the most complex technology of destruction the world has ever known? One objector put it this way: "My advice to every person who signed the peace letter is to become better informed. I have found that nuclear armament/disarmament is not a simple issue." Indeed it is not, and I dare say, most of us who signed that letter make it our business to become as well informed as possible. In fact, it was becoming informed that drove me to help write that letter. But the truth of the nuclear threat is not found in reports that add to our knowledge so much as in stories that make our hearts see.

A mother of a bright fourteen-year-old boy told me that her son had begun to fail in school. She and her husband learned that the boy was experimenting with drugs, and had contemplated suicide. Because the parents loved him very much, they would not rest until they found out the cause of his despair. And it was this: He did not believe that he would ever grow up. He saw the superpowers rattling their weapons at each other, and he lost hope for the world and his own life in the world.

"So I began telling him stories," she told me, "just as I had when he was tiny. I began to tell him stories about himself — about what he would be like when he was an old man." She laughed nervously as she talked. "I felt like a fool — here he was a great hulking kid, bigger than I was, and I was telling him stories. But he wanted to hear them. He was desperate to hear them. I had to give him some hope." I must say parenthetically that this same mother was informing herself and trying to find out what she could do to make that story more than wishful thinking. But the reason I am telling you the story is obvious. If I say to you, "Our children are frightened," you ask me where I get that information. And when I tell you where I get the information, you ask: "Are those studies trustworthy?" Isn't part of the problem that people like you are frightening them? But if you see that fear-sickened fourteen-year-old boy clinging to his mother's descriptions of his eighty-year-old shuffling walk, his false teeth, his spotty memory, his finding a pathetic hope in a vision of his own senility, you can get a glimpse of what the nuclear threat is doing to our children.

It is difficult, if not impossible, to deal directly with the most threatening question of our time. When Dickinson spoke of the dazzling truth that blinded, she was speaking of the kind of truth to which the writer of Exodus was referring. In our time, however, the blinding truth is more likely to be a fireball over the cities of Hiroshima and Nagasaki.

How can we approach this awful reality? In a review of a book of poems about Hiroshima, Terrance DesPres has said: "To questions of this kind there are no answers. Between silence and the scream, any decent heart is trapped."[7]

Yes, I thought, yes, if I am silent, no one will hear; if I scream, no one will listen. So am I trapped? No, not quite. Somewhere lying at a slant between the silence and the scream, there is a story.

We are always at danger when we tackle a poem word by word. Surely, Dickinson means *slant* as *oblique*, as *non-direct*, for she goes on to say, "Success in circuit lies." She's not trying to make us picture a circular slant. But at the risk of pushing the exegesis of the text too far, I want to observe that the word here is *slant*, not *bent*. Now, I am a lover of the poetry of Gerard Manley Hopkins, so when I say *bent,* Hopkins's use of the word springs immediately to mind. He uses *bent* in the sense of *fallen.* The bent world is the one in which man in his arrogance has crushed and defiled nature:

> *Generations have trod, have trod, have trod;*
> *And all is seared with trade; bleared, smeared with toil;*
> *And wears man's smudge and shares man's smell: the soil*
> *Is bare now, nor can foot feel, being shod.*[8]

Related to, but more terrible than, our sins against the natural world is the evil human beings commit against each other. And somehow, because we are human, we seek to justify our unjustifiable actions by telling stories. In this bitter fortieth anniversary marking the end of the Nazi Holocaust, we must force ourselves to remember that Hitler gained power in a depressed and despairing Germany by telling a story. Do you know why our nation is in ruins? he asked. It was the greed of the Jewish financiers and munitions-makers during World War I. Then he went on to tell a story of what Germany really was — a pure Aryan race, destined to be the master race which would conquer the world. And the people believed those bent stories because they wanted a scapegoat for their past misery and a promise for their future.

But how can we test a story to see whether it is bent or slant? In Frank Kermode's *The Sense of an Ending,* he suggests that the difference in the myths of anti-Semitism and, say, the story of *King Lear,* is that the myth of Nazism is a "fiction of escape which tells you nothing about death but projects it onto others; whereas *King Lear* is a fiction that inescapably involves an encounter with oneself, and the image of one's end."[9]

One definition of *bent* reads: "the condition of being deflected, inclined or turned in some other direction" *(Oxford English Dictionary)*. If a story is not a writer's self-judgment, or does not involve the reader in self-judgment but allows both writer and reader to turn that judgment in another direction, we must beware. I suppose I do not have to say how troubled I am with the myths of a righteous, freedom-seeking, peace-keeping America which abound right now. But before I can straighten my country out, I must look to myself. Have I told all the truth, or have I bent my stories?

I once heard Carolyn Forché, the young poet who has written so much about El Salvador, speak on the problem of "political poetry." As Forché pointed out, all poetry, indeed all art, is political with a "soft *p*." Poetry, like fiction, grows out of a particular geographical and political orientation. Artists do not live or work in a vacuum, but in a specific locality during a specific period in history. But there is such a thing, Forché says, as political poetry with a "hard *p*." We recognize this quickly in the kind of poetry that flourished under Stalin — the "Ode to a Wheat Thresher in Siberia" sort of thing. In this kind of political writing, the poet or writer goes to the page with narrowed vision. She knows what she wants to say before she puts it down. The door is closed to her imagination. There are no accidents, no surprises. None could be allowed.

But the true artist comes to the page in service to the work. She does not know, is never sure, because she is always open to accidents. The work informs the artist, not vice versa (from a speech at Old Dominion University, October 1983). This is, of course, why the true artist is seen as a dangerous force in a totalitarian society. If the artist will put her gifts at the disposal of the state, well and good, but if not, she must somehow be neutralized or eliminated.

We in the free world are quite aware of the price that a Pasternak or a Solzhenitsyn must pay. At the same time, we sneer at "art" designed to raise production in a tractor factory in China. But even in free countries, such as ours, and in the field of writing I have chosen, there are still pressures on the writer to be more useful to society — or to some particular segment of our society. We are asked to bend the story in order to blend.

And yet, "A dissonance," William Carlos Williams says in his poem "On the Curies":

> *A dissonance*
> *in the valence of Uranium*
> *led to the discovery*
>
> *Dissonance*
> *(if you're interested)*
> *leads to discovery.*[10]

Writers for children are not asked to bend their stories for evil purposes. The voices that clamor for acknowledgment or preferential treatment are nearly all good. It is not, in nearly every instance, that the cause is not just. And yet, time and again, we refuse to comply. We will insist on putting into our books unpleasant senior citizens, bad-mouthed children, unliberated women, adolescents with uncomfortable sexual feelings, parents who speak ungrammatically. Couldn't we do better? No. I'm afraid not. As Joan Aiken says: ". . . I do not think it is possible to exercise any control over what a creative artist produces, without the risk of wrecking the product. The only possible control," she concludes, "is to shoot the artist."[11]

I think Miss Aiken is right, and just like my little neurotic terrier mutt whose fur bristles on the back of her neck at the least provocation, my fur bristles whenever I hear, or imagine I have heard, someone trying to tell me what I should write. But I suspect I am more sensitive than I need to be. The truth is, I know of few people in this world as free of outside pressures, not to mention control, as I am. The inclination to bend a story — the narrowing of vision — that I must be more careful about does not come from outside myself, but from inside.

I know when I wrote both *The Sign of the Chrysanthemum* and *Of Nightingales That Weep*, I came to those stories without being conscious of a political ax to grind. I was trying to discover the meaning of history for me, not explain it to someone else, young or old.

I remember the flush of surprise I felt as I wrote the scene in *Nightingales* when Takiko goes to see the retired empress, now a shaven nun. The empress says to the girl: "I have been thinking about our nation. It lies wounded, Takiko. Perhaps the wound is mortal. I pray not. But where do we turn for healing? I have learned what my father never knew, that the power of armies can only destroy." And then she answered her own question in a way that quite surprised me: "Do you remember," she asked, "how my mother used to say that your music was better for my son than medicine? Perhaps, Takiko, we are meant to learn that beauty can heal." (p. 167)

I say *surprise,* because I didn't know what the empress meant by *beauty.* I'm still working on it. I get glimpses every now and then, but I'm still stretching toward it. What is beauty, and can it indeed heal in a world where there are Beiruts and Nicaraguas and Northern Irelands and Polands and Afghanistans and South Africas and Ethiopias?

By the time I wrote *The Master Puppeteer,* I had lost my first innocence as a writer. It became harder to come to the paper without being conscious of preconceived notions. I'd moved several hundred years closer to the present. The parallels between eighteenth-century Japan and my own time were more apparent from the outset. And within a year or so of the time I'd written it, I had this to say about it:

> In choosing to tell such a story, I saw that a certain honesty was demanded by history. I could no more prettify the riots of Osaka than I could the riots of Watts or Detroit or Washington. Readers have recoiled from the maiming of Kinshi. The authorities were cruel in eighteenth-century Japan. But during the riots that occurred in Washington . . . there were many voices demanding that the police shoot to kill all looters or *would-be-looters.* Perhaps we haven't moved quite so far from the ancient cruelties as we'd like to think we have.
>
> Perhaps if I can understand why the poor of Osaka felt driven to senseless violence, I will be driven to examine the roots of violence in my own city. Recently my husband was called to the aid of an elderly widow who had a total monthly income of $205, from which she had to hand over $189 to a landlord who lived, as I imagined him, quite comfortably and peacefully in a distant suburb, totally oblivious to the violence that he was inflicting on another human life. Perhaps a reader, though this may be too much to ask, reading of the rice merchants of Osaka, will recognize his own unconscious complicity in the acts of violence committed daily against the poor of the world. But if not the reader, surely the writer.[12]

I was right about one thing when I wrote that. It is too much to ask the reader to see parallels. The only thing a writer can do is tell the story. She had no right to ask the reader to read it in a particular way.

Writing, as I said earlier, echoing Ibsen, is self-judgment. If a particular novel or poem or story pronounces judgment on the society in which the writer lives, it must do so because the writer is a part of that society and she has in this writing searched her own soul.

As I listened to Carolyn Forché talk about political poetry, I asked myself whether my political *p*s had been hard or soft. I couldn't answer the question when it came to *Rebels of the Heavenly Kingdom*. This book comes closer to our time than any of the other historical fiction I have written, and I am still too close to the actual writing of it. One reviewer said, "I haven't read any book in years that seemed more clearly contemporary." [13] I think she meant it as a compliment, but I had to wonder if it also indicated a hardening of the political intent. Had I come to that book with my vision narrowed, knowing before I began what it was that I wanted to say?

But whatever faults the book might have, I remember the great surprise that it gave me — the accident that for me, the writer, breathed life into the story.

It was the character of San-niang. The general of the horsewomen is based on a historical character who was perhaps, in fact, the sister of the cruel Western king. There is not a great deal said about her otherwise, except that she was the leader of the horsewomen, who, arrayed in gorgeous tunics and trousers, brought terror to their superstitious enemies. The Manchu armies saw in these horsewomen the return of the women warriors of legend.

San-niang thundered into my story riding bareback, an illiterate, superstitious, big-footed peasant, and became for me the heart of the tragedy that was the Taiping Tienkuo — the Heavenly Kingdom of Great Peace.

> On horseback, San-niang looked like a warrior goddess of the ancient stories. Her long black hair streamed out behind her like a banner as she rode. There was no saddle, only two narrow strips of rein. San-niang let these lie across her hand, barely holding them at all. "We must command with our bodies," she explained. "Our hands must be free for the bow." Back and forth through the length of the narrow gorge she rode. Mei Lin, watching her diminish into the distance, held her breath. Somehow she feared that the tiny horse and rider might, on reaching the farther end, take off into the sky like an eagle soaring high over the mountains, never to return. But each time, the figure — for horse and woman were one being, there at the limit of her vision — would arc until now it was flying toward her, growing in size and power and loveliness as it came. "She is mortal just as I am. She is my barefoot sister from Thistle Mountain." Mei Lin pulled a piece of wild grass and sucked its bitter stem. It was the only thing that tasted of reality.[14]

This may sound strange to you, coming from the writer, but I love San-niang as though she were someone I was privileged to know, not as a character who sprang mostly from my imagination. If Wang Lei and Mei Lin, who are the central characters of this book, say something about the person I think I am, San-niang, like Maime Trotter before her, says something about the person I wish I were. And I mourn for San-niang very much in the same way that I mourn for Leslie Burke. For, unlettered peasant that she was, she fought gallantly for what she believed in, and, when her cause betrayed her, she gave her life and liberty for those she loved.

If it is clear, then, that a story should not project blame or seek to manipulate the reactions of the reader, that a story should not be bent or seek to bend, what should it be?

I was afraid you'd ask that. Well, let me throw some ideas at you for lack of a proper definition. When I am involved in telling a story, I am involved in an experience that controls me, rather than vice versa. Each story has its own life, its own rhythm, its own color. That is why *Come Sing, Jimmy Jo* bears very little resemblance to *Of Nightingales That Weep*. Writing a novel demands patience on my part, because when I begin, I don't know this story. I've never heard it before. I gradually come to know it as I live with it over a period of time. The story teaches me how it must be told. So the first thing a story is, is itself — a unique, harmonious whole. But this whole is not inert. Within this whole there is movement and growth. When I first began to write stories, there was a little jingle that would ring in my head. "Something's got to happen. Someone's got to change." Now, that was wise advice, as jingles go, but what it didn't say was that movement and growth by themselves are not enough. The movement and growth in a story has to be structured. It has to be part of the harmony of the whole. It can't be senseless or random, the way reality seems to be. It has to provide within the harmony of the whole a unifying and life-giving function — like blood and nerves and muscles in the human body. And when a story is unified and alive, it can give life and unity to the reader.

The truth, Barry Lopez reminds us in an essay on narrative fiction, is not something that can be "explicitly stated" or "reduced to aphorism or formulas. It is something alive and unpronounceable. Story creates a pattern in which [truth] can reveal itself." Of course, this is the point I was trying to make earlier, but I come back to it, because Lopez goes on to talk about the positive function of narrative, which I spoke of earlier in a more negative way as self-judgment, but which he says is to "nurture and heal, to repair a spirit in disarray." Literature is important, he says, insofar as it sustains us "with illumination and heal[s] us." [15]

My husband and I have four children. One day fifteen years ago, the baby, a dimpled, loving darling who worshipped her father, turned to him and said loudly and with passion: "No!" Her father looked at me with anguish in his face. "We're not going to have to go through this with Mary, too, are we?" Yes, with Mary, too. Now Mary is seventeen, and we are, for the fourth time, going through solo driving, waiting up at night, and an English course entitled "Literary Analysis."

For the fourth time a child of mine is coming to me and saying: "Mom, when a writer writes all that stuff down, they don't know what it means, do they?"

"No," I confess each time, feeling a bit like a literary anarchist.

"We're supposed to find all these symbols and explain them. I bet the writers don't even know they're in there, right?"

"If they do," I mumble unhappily, "they're probably not very good writers."

"Then how come I have to study this stuff?"

My impulse is to yell: "So you can get an academic

diploma!" But all four times I have managed to restrain myself. It's a mercy I don't have five children.

If you ask me what one of my stories is about, I will sputter and stammer and, depending on how self-controlled I am, either give you a very childish answer: "Well, it's about this girl who's jealous of her sister." Or I will cry out: "If I could tell you what it was about in one sentence, why would I have spent nearly three years and two hundred and fifteen pages to do so?" In the writer's mind, her story is not divisible, explainable, reduceable. "Some people," Flannery O'Connor says, "have the notion that you read the story and then climb out of it into the meaning, but for the fiction writer himself the whole story is the meaning, because it is an experience, not an abstraction."[16]

I was asked not long ago to be my own critic, to write an article for a literary journal discussing the religious symbols that occur in my work. Now, I would be surprised, not to say disturbed, if there were no religious symbols lurking about in my books. But to go poking around for them, separating them from the flesh of the story — I'd almost sooner have my own cadaver cut open and the various organs exposed and prodded by a first-year medical student.

I'm not speaking here about your task as reader or critic or teacher. Our calling is not the same. You may very well have to teach my child literary analysis with the hope that she may learn to read with care and understanding and, I pray, appreciation and joy. I notice, moreover, that even a hypersensitive storyteller like myself can be persuaded to analyze other people's books for a small monetary consideration. That's the reviewer and critic's task, and it is different from the task of the writer. But even as we analyze, we must never lose sight of the whole. For it is the work in its wholeness, not the chewed-up bits and pieces, that "sustains us with illumination."

I refused earlier this spring to watch the latest dramatization of *Anna Karenina,* because the local reviewer revealed the fact that Levin had been left out of the story. Well, you can't have *Anna Karenina* and leave out Levin. It just doesn't work. All you have left is another adultery gone sour, and you can get that every Friday night on *Dallas.* You don't have Tolstoy's experience of truth.

At a lower level, a librarian friend of mine confessed that she tried to read *The Great Gilly Hopkins* aloud while doing a running censorship of all the profanities. So, for example, Gilly says "Rats!" to which Trotter solemnly replies: "We don't take the name of the Lord in vain around here." You see the problem.

A story that is any good is all of a piece. We can turn it about and look at it from different angles; better yet, we can get inside it and let it look at us; but when we start abstracting its meanings or pulling out bits that don't happen to suit our fancy, we diminish the story's power to illumine truth for us.

And what about the power of the story to heal, to, as Barry Lopez says, "repair a spirit in disarray"? I realize I must tackle the subject of healing very carefully. I do not have to tell you how desperately the world needs healing, how disarrayed, indeed how broken are the spirits of nearly everyone we meet. I don't want you to think that I regard writers as literary paramedics who rush about applying tourniquets to the bleeding wounds of the world. If it were only so simple.

In a newspaper essay I wrote for *The Virginian Pilot* in 1984, I asked the rhetorical question, How do you write a book for children who do not know if there will be a world for them to grow up in? I got an answer in an irate letter to the editor: "Easy, lady. You don't! Leave the writing to someone who knows that children need to enjoy life as children and not have their childhood stolen from them. If you can't do that, don't write at all."

Now, I have a lot of problems with this statement, in addition to my obvious reluctance to give up my life's work. The first problem is with the narrowness of this gentleman's concern. He is not talking about those thousands of children who died or who were permanently injured from the noxious fumes of a Union Carbide plant, or those who lie with bloated bellies in dusty camps in Ethiopia, those children who die daily in dirty little wars, or those who are beaten or cursed or neglected. He is talking about his children and mine — bright, handsome, winsome, healthy, self-confident. Children who have never felt the sting of prejudice, who laugh freely and bring their parents joy — a tiny minority of all the children who live out their lives in this world. And yet, even these, the super-blessed, cannot be left to enjoy a childhood isolated from the pain and grief and horror of the real world. The world is too much with us. Even our most cared-for and most deeply loved are often trapped between silence and the scream.

I think the reason these children like my books is because they know that I take their feelings and their fears seriously. They, the tiny minority of the blessed, still need stories that are both an illumination and a healing.

The word *heal* means to make whole. This is more than patching up, it is more than simply catharsis, the purging of the emotions. We are concerned here with growing, with becoming. We don't come into this world fully human. We become human, we become whole. And contrary to what our President might imply, stories are not frills in the curriculum of life. They are vital nourishment in this process of becoming fully human, of becoming whole.

I think of the books that started me on the road to becoming human and I am awed and grateful. *The House at Pooh Corner; The Wind in the Willows; The Secret Garden; The Good Master; Peter Rabbit; Little Women; Heidi; Paddle to the Sea; The Yearling; A Tale of Two Cities; Cry the Beloved Country;* and, of course, the Bible. I am troubled by those who feel they must tailor their publishing list or their acquisitions to "what children like." How do you know what you like when you're eight or ten? You're still at the early end of the process of becoming human. We don't bow to our children's whims when it comes to physical nourishment. I don't know of any mothers who buy only sugared cereals and bubble gum for fear of imposing their own adult tastes on their impressionable young.

I don't mean for a minute that we should dose our young with mournful tales, much less better them with brutalizing ones. Surely laughter is necessary for wholeness and calculated shock a disintegrating, rather than a nurturing, experience.

It is the task of stories, by the harmony of their vision, to help us find our own connections within and without. They should provide us occasions to judge ourselves, and they should nourish us that we may grow even more human. They should, at their very best, give us a glimpse of the backside of glory.

In an essay in *The New York Times,* Kathryn Morton

addresses the question of the function of fiction and concludes:

> More than just show us order in hypothetical existences, novelists give us demonstration classes in what is the ultimate work of us all, for by days and years we must create the narrative of our own lives. A pawky, artless mess we easily make of it. We prewrite Great Drama, and then, pressed for time, dash off any old thing for the published version. We labor over and constantly revise the past and the present, Monday morning quarterbacking our way through the week to find unifying principles and meaning. We hope for some pleasant repeating themes, and pray that, when finished, the whole may have something of beauty in it. It is lonely work; we are all amateurs. To glance up and see a great novelist offering a story of rare, sweet wit and grace is to feel that our heart has found its home.
>
> So you say that reading a novel is a way to kill time when the real world needs tending to. I tell you that the only world I know is the world *as* I know it, and I am still learning how to comprehend that. These books are showing me ways of being I could never have managed alone. I am not killing time, I'm trying to make a life.[17]

To illumine and make whole — I am not equal to the commission, but at least I know how important the task is, and even if the world today reverences and rewards those who make and possess the largest, sharpest rocks, I'm grateful to be in the long line of those who, reaching to be human, have gathered their children about the fire and told them stories.

NOTES

1. Katherine Paterson, *The Great Gilly Hopkins* (New York: Crowell, 1978), p. 148.
2. Carl T. Rowan column, North America Syndicate, September, 1984.
3. Jacob Bronowski, *The Origins of Knowledge and the Imagination* (New Haven, CT: Yale University Press, 1978), pp. 36 ff.
4. ———, "The Reach of the Imagination," *Norton Reader* (New York: Norton, 1980), p. 105.
5. *The Complete Works of Emily Dickinson* (Boston: Little, Brown, 1951), poem number 1129.
6. Reprinted in program note for an amateur production and attributed simply to *The New York Times*.
7. Terrance DesPres, *American Book Review*, January/February 1985.
8. Gerard Manley Hopkins, "God's Grandeur." *The Poems of Gerard Manley Hopkins*, ed. W. H. Gardner and N. H. MacKenzie (London: Oxford University Press, 1970), p. 66.
9. Frank Kermode, *The Sense of an Ending* (New York: Oxford University Press, 1966), p. 39.
10. William Carlos Williams, "On the Curies." *Paterson* Book IV (New York: New Directions, 1963), p. 176.
11. Joan Aiken, quoted in *Children and Literature,* ed., Virginia Haviland (New York: Lothrop, 1973), p. 149.
12. Katherine Paterson, *Gates of Excellence* (New York: Elsevier-Nelson, 1981).
13. Kathryn Morton, *The Virginian-Pilot,* May 29, 1983.
14. Katherine Paterson, *Rebels of the Heavenly Kingdom* (New York: Dutton, 1983), pp. 109–110.
15. Barry Lopez, *Harper's,* December 1984, p. 52.
16. Flannery O'Connor, *Mystery and Manners* (New York: Farrar, Straus & Giroux, 1961), p. 73.
17. Kathryn Morton, *The New York Times,* December 23, 1984.

Introduction to Virginia Hamilton

WHEN I FIRST MET Virginia Hamilton, it was in 1974, right after she won the triple crown — the Newbery, Boston Globe–Horn Book, and National Book Awards — for her novel, *M. C. Higgins the Great*. She asked me, in all innocence I presume, what was so different about her books. It was a justifiable question, since all the starred reviews said her books were different. I fumbled toward something about imagination and originality, but it wasn't a very satisfactory answer, and I've thought about it a lot over a score of years as I've read each of her books. Although imagination and originality are always rare commodities, other writers of children's literature do have them. There's something more specific about Virginia's work which, if I can finally define it, I would call a joining of the traditional and the innovative to make strong new literary structures.

Her Jahdu tales use words in rhythmic patterns of folkloric storytelling that are renewed to fit and follow the small roving rascal who dares to come from a mythical past, even as far as the streets of Harlem — Jahdu, whose favorite word as he runs in and out of trouble is *Woogily*, an exclamation that will stand by any child in times of trouble. The heroine of *Zeely* assumes the image of a Watusi queen who seems to walk out of an African past into the present, just as a mysterious figure in *The House of Dies Drear* emerges from the days of slavery into the lives of a midwestern family. *Arilla Sun Down* explores a girl's African American and Native American roots in a stream-of-consciousness narrative. *The Magical Adventures of Pretty Pearl* blends mythology and history with a god-child's wandering from Mount Kenya, where she lived with her brother John de Conquer, down through the world and woods of the American South, into hiding with black and Cherokee refugees, into the company of the giant hero John Henry himself. *Willie Bea and the Time the Martians Landed* returns to the dynamics of an extended family on a specific night — Halloween of 1938, during Orson Welles's famous broadcast. The protagonist of *M. C. Higgins the Great* struggles to unite a legacy of hill-country music and community with commercial invasions that loom in a slag heap over his future. *Sweet Whispers Brother Rush* materializes a family ghost to help a child understand her neglectful mother and dying brother. Even the realistic novel *A Little Love* connects the relationship of a young couple with that of grandparents, so that the sense of personality as history is never lost. *The Planet of Junior Brown* deals with the sorrows of children who have been cut off from their roots, the bare emotional survival of those who must substitute peer for generational support. Hamilton's complex biographies of Paul Robeson and W. E. B. Du Bois strengthen young people's understanding of parallel conflicts in their society's past.

Virginia Hamilton's recharging of tradition with currents of creative energy and untried techniques carries literature from the past through the hands of the living present into a lasting future. What child can resist this cumulatively cadenced retelling from *The People Could Fly: American Black Folktales*? Like most of her writing, it will sound both deeply familiar and strikingly new.

Little Daughter was outside the fence now. She saw another pretty flower. She skipped over and got it, held it in her hand. It smelled sweet. She saw another and she got it, too. Put it with the others. She was makin a pretty bunch to put in her vase for the table. And so Little Daughter got farther and farther away from the cabin. She picked the flowers, and the whole time she sang a sweet song.

All at once Little Daughter heard a noise. She looked up and saw a great big wolf. The wolf said to her, in a low gruff voice, said, "Sing that sweetest, goodest song again."

So the little girl sang it, sang,

"Tray-bla, tray-bla, cum qua, kimo."

And, *pit-a-pat, pit-a-pat, pit-a-pat, pit-a-pat,* Little Daughter tiptoed toward the gate. She's goin back home. But she hears big and heavy, PIT-A-PAT, PIT-A-PAT, comin behind her. And there's the wolf. He says, "Did you move?" in a gruff voice.

Little Daughter says, "Oh, no, dear wolf, what occasion have I to move?"

"Well, sing that sweetest, goodest song again," says the wolf.

Little Daughter sang it:

"Tray-bla, tray-bla, cum qua, kimo."

And the wolf is gone again.

The child goes back some more, *pit-a-pat, pit-a-pat, pit-a-pat,* softly on tippy-toes toward the gate.

But she soon hears very loud, PIT-A-PAT, PIT-A-

PAT, comin behind her. And there is the great big wolf, and he says to her, says, "I think you moved."

"Oh, no, dear wolf," Little Daughter tells him, "what occasion have I to move?"

So he says, "Sing that sweetest, goodest song again."

Little Daughter begins:

"Tray-bla, tray-bla, tray-bla, cum qua, kimo."

The wolf is gone.

But, PIT-A-PAT, PIT-A-PAT, PIT-A-PAT, comin on behind her. There's the wolf. He says to her, says, "You moved."

She says, "Oh, no, dear wolf, what occasion have I to move?"

"Sing that sweetest, goodest song again," says the big, bad wolf.

She sang:

"Tray bla-tray, tray bla-tray, tray-bla-cum qua, kimo."

The wolf is gone again.

And she, Little Daughter, *pit-a-pat, pit-a-pat, pit-a-pattin* away home. She is so close to the gate now. And this time she hears PIT-A-PAT, PIT-A-PAT, PIT-A-PAT, comin on *quick* behind her.

Little Daughter slips inside the gate. She shuts it — CRACK! PLICK! — right in that big, bad wolf's face.

She sweetest, goodest safe![1]

Virginia Hamilton.

Virginia Hamilton

Hagi, Mose, and Drylongso
May 2, 1986

It is an honor to be here to give the 1986 Zena Sutherland Lecture. There had to have been an occasion when I first met Zena Sutherland, for it was the time I was beginning in my field and had gained some attention for my first book. Thus, I was being shown around and found myself at a festive gathering that included Mrs. Sutherland.

Yet, it is far easier for me to believe that I have always known her than to recall our being introduced. There are persons who affect one significantly. Zena Sutherland has been for me a constant guardian wisely giving advice most often by means of her subtle reviews of many of my books. The best critic, in my opinion, is the one who teaches. I have studied her reviews of my work as one takes a course in How to Build a Fiction. Lesson Number One: Never paint the *would* until the *could* is nailed. The reviews have been consistently enlightening. It is through educators such as Zena Sutherland that we writers are able to face our weaknesses. Some of us admit, in a moment of weakness, to having them. We trust best the objective, cool hand. At least I do. I recall the last line of Zena's *Bulletin* review of *Arilla Sun Down* in November 1976. She thought that what was outstanding about the book was the characterization and "the dramatic impact of some of the episodes." Now, if the author has any sense, she will key in on the word *some*. She will march right back through the book and ferret out the *other* that may not have had dramatic impact. *Some* does imply *other*. Thank you, Zena, for all that you have taught me over the years.

I will tell you some of the reasons I do my work the way that I do. A novelist writes carrying a single idea, high above her head, like a big stick, over months and months. I have carried a somewhat abstract idea about the fundamentals of writing around for years. Beings, humans, are the long and the short of things. Nothing is beyond the evidence of the senses of beings. That which is being will become, and becoming is everything in terms of the fiction I write. What is lasting and what is permanent is change. That is why novel-writing is my fulfillment. Novel-writing for young people, as opposed to adult novel-writing, presupposes becoming and change. Our young protagonist begins ill-defined, but begin she or he must, whether or not she or he has definition. We observe, reading, as this being changes to become the very embodiment of growth, development, and definition.

A fiction is still a lie, and character, a being, or protagonist in a fiction, is still a set-up, a proof in the air outlined by the imaginative use of language. A fiction doesn't necessarily reflect a real world. It, itself, isn't real. It is a closed system of the author's own creation in which the author "be's" the creator, something of a godperson who must always stand away, out of sight and out of mind as the creation works its way around the undefined being.

The creation encloses the being character in its own unreal world, which for us readers, of course, becomes the only reality. We can't get out of the unreal real world until we put the book down, until the undefined being totally becomes, breaking the bubble, the skin of the creation, of the lie, and we are let go.

The best search for becoming that I have done as the writer, and the best unreal world that I have created is the world and characters of *The Magical Adventures of Pretty Pearl*. I say "the best," because writing the book did best for me what I demanded of myself. I had a picture of a would-be world that I wanted to have become a real world. I wrote as near to the picture as I could. So *The Magical Adventures* begins as one thing and ends by becoming another. The merging of being and becoming is here as close as I've ever written. The novelist working within this fiction *fragments* herself into separate *entities* or qualities that become creators of the unfolding fiction. High John de Conquer and John Henry, existing as they do ready-made in black myth and lore, are two sides of a gold coin kept spinning in the same way that the totally imagined Mother Pearl and Pretty Pearl are two sides of another coin. Here is a whirling, blinding balance of natural forces.

The Magical Adventures is at once my most fun and most serious work. It is an organic whole coming as it does from the depths of the author-creator. There are mistakes, of course, errors of judgment and choices — all of my books have them. Perhaps all books have them to some extent. The dialect or speech is off-putting for some black people, particularly, and for high-school-age students who, having less historical perspective, misread the colloquial speech of *The Magical Adventures* as stereotypical black English. If I had a second chance, I might think about doing the language differently. But aesthetically, I think the language is true within the confines of the would-be world of the book.

A really first-rate lie that passes itself off as a fiction should reveal a clear face-to-face stand between illusion and reality. I think of illusion as the art of the impression of being. The art of fiction or literature is the illusion of reality. The magical effects that change Pretty Pearl into Mother Pearl are the art of illusion at work on character, atmosphere, and place.

Reality can be thought of as time, movement, action, *becoming*. Reality is change inside the illusion of reality. Perhaps all is illusion after all. This kind of thinking reveals that our very words become illusive. Our language — *all is illusion after all* — becomes ephemeral. The perfect book would be one in which each word vanishes as it is read. This mental exercise, a kind of intellectual strip-tease, often brings me insight into some fiction I'm working on. I want us to rid ourselves of any set, easy pieces we may have and allow our minds to open and our feelings to rise.

When I finish a book, I get rid of most of the imaginative residue and real research by simply putting the residue out of my mind, forgetting it, and by laying aside the tangible evidence. Presently, the tangible evidence, including drafts of a book, becomes the Virginia Hamilton papers and are shipped off to Kent State and Central State Universities in Ohio, which keep my papers for scholars and students. When the material of a book is laid out from beginning to end, it can be a revelation to researchers, other working writers, and even to me — how bad a first draft was and how it finally evolved into something decent. When I look at this material again after many years, I don't remember what my thinking was when I wrote it. But once I start reading, I can get back into the imaginative processes fairly easily.

Although my involvement with *The People Could Fly* is over, I am holding on to much of the research, at least the pieces of it, the flavor, place, and time, in order to maintain the same mental state of the plantation era for another project I'm attempting. This involves a time period one hundred and thirty years ago, and we can call it a docu-novel, something based on factual material and historical incidents, but with blank areas that can only be filled with fiction.

At the same time, I am working on a contemporary young adult novel in which the black female protagonist idealizes her newfound friends, a nitty-gritty young white couple whom she actually nicknames "A White Romance," which is also the title of the book. Again, in the abstract, it is a story of illusion scraping against reality that demonstrates further the act of being and becoming. However, I do not write in the abstract, although I think in it, and this book is written on a very down-to-earth level to reveal a young black woman seeing a white world, a white romance, in her own cultural and racial terms.

The People Could Fly was one of those thoroughly pleasurable projects that one comes upon occasionally. The book wasn't my idea. It was my publisher who said to me, only you, Virginia, can do this project justice and only the Dillons can illustrate it. I was convinced in less than two seconds that this was absolutely true. It was a project that

I could work on maybe eight, ten hours a day without really feeling that I had left the swing and the playground. If I discovered a clue to something, I couldn't stop until I had tracked down the solution. And it didn't feel like work; it felt like an exploration of my own heart and being.

My initial plan for the book was like a puzzle. I could work at it in parts and then put all of the parts together. The title and the title story, "The People Could Fly," were with me from the beginning. This tale came to mind when the project was proposed to me, and it became my barometer and the yardstick by which I measured the atmosphere and depth of other tales and how they might fit into the whole scheme. If a tale didn't fit easily into my puzzle with "The People Could Fly" as the centerpiece, then I decided not to use it.

Now that the book is out there in the real world and all of us who worked on it are long since finished with it, I feel as though *The People Could Fly* is truly free at last. It has found its own level. It has soared. It appears to have a very broad appeal, and a writer can ask for nothing better for one of her books. So much is lost, thrown away over and over again in our society. Maybe this book will become a bridge from one time to another.

Black people themselves continue to rediscover their own history. I have had people tell me that *The People Could Fly* literally changed their lives. We tend to think that everyone is like ourselves, continually involved with literature and history. It is always a marvel to discover that there are people who live in this world only reading books very occasionally. A book like *The People Could Fly* makes a profound impression on the intermittent reader.

Working in the area of black history and experience can be sobering at times. It is always thought-provoking. It is often exciting. I have never found the material of black heritage and culture a cause for despair. One feels like a detective, many times, tracking along the "hopesteps" of beings dead and gone. Following trails of dogged courage and will beyond imagining across dangerous entrapments.

One never knows what one will discover alone at night, steeped in the research. I do start working very early in the morning. By nightfall, if the world is really evolving — that is, if my mind is working — I may cease to feel as though I am body. I become mind and idea, response and feeling. I am free of my time and place. I am one of the long-gone beings come back to life there in my study, which itself expands into a road, a path, a darkness, a world. Cunning, desperate, beyond alertness, I am *being* this hearing-intense individual, all-seeing in the dark.

One night I took a side trip, following a mere mention of a group of African Americans who escaped hard ground together. In the dark, they ran, some thirty of them, mostly adults and strong male children. They went a long way, long time, and I followed. The first one held tightly to the hand of the second, and so on. There was no leader. There was just the first, the second, on down the line. Long, long time, and finally, they crossed a great river. They were free. They had hidden so well, had run into no other humans, had made their way over weeks and weeks without speaking more than a few words to the fugitive behind or in front.

At last, they straggled out of hiding. They saw people. But sadly, they could not understand a word spoken. Evidently it happened that, in their confusion of days and nights of wandering, they had got turned around. They'd crossed the wrong river. This was not the Ohio River. For the place was Mexico, and the river turned out to be the Rio Grande.

What an extraordinary tale for a collector of tales to stumble upon. Perhaps some of you know about this historical incident. The account that I've told you is all that I've found. I made note of the incident and put it away. Then I neglected to note where I put my reminder of the source material, carelessness which is typical of me when I'm distracted. Oh, I'll remember, I tell myself.

But what happened to those people? What year was it? Did they all survive? What, where, when? Sometimes it's hard to let something like that go. I think about it at odd moments. I don't go looking for the material. Maybe someday there will be time for that special hunt.

The period of slavocracy and abolition, masters and servants, rivers and runaways, and bounty hunters and rendition stays with me because of my work on the new docunovel and because that period of history always gives me new insights. Sometimes, the research takes me back beyond what I actually need for my story. Often, it is necessary to divine what is in a name or a song or a saying. Figure out why these bonded ones were so certain that there was a time when animals talked, for instance. One finds very general references in the research for such a time, just as one finds fragments about flying and flying Africans and empty fields in which the farm tools continue to work with nary a hand to move them.

Perhaps Hagi knew of this, and Mose, and that the time was Drylongso. A long time ago, imagine you could be there on the cleared land, perhaps a thousand acres surrounded by the miles-wide bands of impenetrable forests.

The dead silence rises from the clods of earth as a condition of dreadful soundlessness.

The heat surrounds everything, smothering like a shroud. The stench hangs above the heat shroud, spreading like a curse. It is the odor of decay and animal and human waste, of climatic inversions that hold the putrid smell of the unwashed who have sweated, slaved, slept, sweated, awakened, sweated, and gone unwashed for days and weeks and months. The stench is a bitter taste, settled down in the soured lunch pails, eaten and swallowed by the hundreds of the slaving in the endless rows as the sorrowful nourishment of their days. There are too many of these blacks, finally; there is too much cotton and the price, too low, too much heat and stench. Only the bonded can withstand such heat and the diseases that rise out of it. At any given time in the heat months, a fourth of them are sick. Who is there to remark on their being born and dying? Only they, themselves.

The owners are gone from the plantation. They have taken to the forests—lock, stock, and slave guards to watch their children, and servants to prepare and hand them their food. They will stay among the cool forest trees in their summer dwellings for the duration of the devil months, to return when the weather breaks around harvesttime; the only whites remaining to watch over the fields and the blacks are the overseers.

Overseer turns red, angry from the broiling sun. He grinds his hate through the rawhide whip slashes at black shoulders. The driver remains, as well, for he and his family, if he's got one, are the only black elite allowed on the plantation, with his home away from the other slave quarters and next to the overseer's.

The little-known driver, the overseer's right hand, was always a black man, the strongest and baddest — John Henry would have made a typical one, if he'd got knocked out of him his tender heart. The driver was able to handle rawhide even better than the overseer. Caught in the middle between slaves and masters, he was perhaps the first one called Mose, feared by ordinary slaves more than they feared the overseer who was the man's substitute. The driver was made to dress differently from the slaves, so that he could always be identified with the overseer, the stand-in man.

If the driver turned on the stand-in man, then the overseer would, in turn, turn on the slaves. But if the driver turned against his own kind, then he had done the dirty work for the man, himself. And if the driver could relent and fool the stand-in man, then, he would. But if he could not, the driver would do what he must to those of his kind and to himself. He was the slave driver, a tribute unto himself. No slave was ever more alone and hidden inside himself than was the driver, at once victim and victimized. In that great tale, "The People Could Fly," in the end, it is the overseer who tells about the flying Africans. It is the master who says it is all a lie and a trick of the light. But it is the driver who keeps his mouth shut.

Driver blows his horn or rings a bell after all hands have eaten the evening meal. "Oh, yes! Oh, yes! Ev'body in an' the doors locked,"[2] he hollers, signaling from the quarter to the overseer the end of both the slaves' labors and the quick moments of time available for the family and the social life on the slave street. Driver is responsible for so much — for sweeping the neighborhood for runaways, and the nightly verbal report to the overseer of the day's accomplishments and failures. He might lose his position at any time if he didn't do well, to end a beast of burden back in the fields.

See how overrun the fields are with this bent-low, squat-low humanity? They are better than cattle or horses, for they know how to straighten and ease their spines. They know how to laugh and sing, how to hold back the fear and the crying, and how to pick and pluck in unison. The more of us be, the quicker we work, they once thought. But why work quick, they learned, when there is no pay for anything? And if *They* find out there's no work for us to do, we'll get sold. Then where will we be? No one knows how bad a new owner, worse than one we have.

The women in their own cotton field, endless rows. The men in separate fields, hour upon hour. All these are the ones who labor on down to earth. These are the sorry ones who do not know the magic, that special African mystery. They cannot fly; cannot flee. They have no idea where they are, save that it is never home. It is called Partee Plantation, or Boyntin. They don't know where to run. See the blackness all around, and how far is the far over there where the horizon meets the forests? Only the owner and his tribe may enter the forest, so he says. But old Hagi and some of the others know better.

Hagi watches. Hagi, the granddaughter of an old driver, ancient herself now. Her work is valuable, although less each year. But she is ready with the tools of her trade, pieces of towels, some clear water for the brow. Sure hands and healing roots. A knife for cutting what must be severed. If a woman looks to fall with a borning child, Hagar is quick to scrape a hole over which the pregnant one will crouch and drop the babe. But right now, all is calm. Hagar, called Hagi, straightens her coarse sackcloth.

She stands, shields her eyes, looks off into the unending paleness of the sizzling light. Up there in the blinding blue shines even brighter the one called Hannah, that burning being sun.

"Huh," Hagi grunts. Shielding her eyes, she purses her lips and whistles in a piercing scream that is like a soul lost on the air. All others in the fields pause as the whistle screams by them, then ceases. It is a signal, and the sound of Hagi's voice now rises on the stillness.

The field hands, as little as one-fourth hands, boys and girls of thirteen; half hands, older youngsters; three-quarter hands, young, strong women; and whole hands, either one man in his prime or a prime man and his woman — they sway with this ancient formula for bringing life: Hagar's song.

> *Blow winds, Blow winds blow,*
> *Wind, blow winds, blow.*
> *Oh, won't you go down Hannah,*
> *Sunlight*
> *Drylongso, Drylongso!*

Strong Mose, grandson of drivers and cousin to old Hagi, is there in the field with the men. He catches the whistle first. Listens for the incantation. Hears it and takes it up, carrying it deep inside, and brings it forth again in his male strength to the other men: "You go down, now, Hannah, Oh, Hannah!"

Hagar's lament was a message, telling all who cared where they would meet in secret. For it was forbidden for more than five of them to meet together. Absolutely forbidden that they enter the forest. Never would they murmur or even think their own names or the names of those who would gather.

But "Hannah go down," was the key phrase. Sundown brought darkness and darkness was the forest. *Drylongso* was the word.

They did meet way in the dark deep in the forest trees. And the password was given, barely whispered, "Drylongso." And answered, "Drylongso." Right there in the dark, where one could not see another, where there was safety in invisibility. And they would ask of one another, "That you, Possum?"

"Yay," Ol' Possum would answer.

And "That you, Sis Goose?"

"Ayay, Ayay, hit's me. And you, Bruh Bear?"

"Yayo, it's me, it's me."

And on around in the dark. "That you, Bruh Rabbit?"

"Nobody else but," says the Rabbit.

"What you got to tell tonight?" asks Bruh Deer.

"That you, Deer?"

"Aye, me, and Allugatah right by me."

"Well," the Rabbit says. "Come tell my dream, call it war or free-dom."

"Well which?"

"Don't know, but just got to tell."

"Wait," Sis Goose says. "First, where be Bruh Fox?"

"Bruh Fox," Old Possum says way low, "he gone."

"He gone?"

"Yay, fox done flew the coop. He done run the run. Fox gone and gone the long, long gone."

"Ayay. Ayay."

So, therefore, begins the time the animals talked. A brief docudrama. This, then, is the beginning of being and my being. Now we surmise, we infer how and why the animals talked, and how so many animal tales came to be. The slaves deliberately took on the names and personalities of the animals of the plantation as a cover to protect themselves even from themselves during those dangerous, clandestine meetings by which they passed along plantation knowledge, knowledge of the world, of the forest and beyond, where they told tales and truths about matters that concerned their survival.

Conjecture rises from the actual source material like a mist. The people I create move through the mist, dignified, dramatic, isolated, universal, forever made different and the same, yet always human and always changing.

I imagine that Hagi, as they called her, overheard the mistress say something to the effect that, "Mistress believe the rain done dried up, the world be dry so long."

Now Hagar heard these words, exactly as they were said — dry so long. But she knew *drought* in her own words, her own language structures handed down, from near-myths handed out of old Africa, from the bowed humanity in the holds of slave ships. She could smell *stepney,* they called drought and hunger, in the very air, years before it came. And stepney slowly became for her drylongso. It was black people hungry and thirsty. Drylongso had been lived with and dealt with for as long as anyone could remember.

When the anthropologist John Langston Gwaltney published his self-portrait of Black America entitled *Drylongso* in 1980, one of his contributors said this about herself:

> I know your mother must have told you what mine told me: "The tongue is steel, but a closed mouth is a shield."
> You know, I said that to that child and she got out

her little book and wrote it down. I like that child because she's what I was when I was young. I don't mean I look like her. The truth is, son, I have never been the kind of person people would turn around and look at in the street. I'm just, well, what you might say drylongso. Neither ugly nor pretty, just drylongso.[3]

Drylongso came to mean ordinary, the way drought was not news in Africa or in America. It is only natural that those driven by drought should become one and the same with it. Ordinary. Drylongso.

Clarence Major's *Dictionary of Afro-American Slang,* published by International Publishers in 1970, designates *drylongso* as three separate words, and defines it as a 1940s expression meaning dullness or fate.

I have studied enough black dialect and true narrative to know that slang expressions existing in the forties were likely current in the thirties and collected in WPA projects. Much of the narrative was related by actual former slave informants or their immediate descendants. I find it remarkable that drylongso is in current usage. Just as are Hagar and Mose. Hagar, or Hagi, being the archetypal, mythic black elder woman of the so-called American Black nation. The character Hagar is a key figure in Toni Morrison's *Song of Solomon.* Mose has been always the prototype for the ordinary or common black male. He is the former driver or his descendant who, by his bravery and caring, has fallen from the governor's grace to the level of the ordinary field hand.

The Dictionary of Afro-American Slang defines Mose as simply "A Negro." Gwaltney calls Mose the archetypal "straight" black male. The typical Mose in one of my books would be Black Salt from *The Magical Adventures* or perhaps Silversmith from *Sweet Whispers Brother Rush*.

The Black Salt character is at once ordinary and extraordinary. Of the people, he has the driver's leadership ability as well as the patriarch's desire to protect and lead his kind. Silversmith is a protector, also, for young Teresa Pratt, a father figure with the common touch.

The younger female or the young woman of the black nation has numerous names. Pretty Pearl and Mother Pearl from *The Magical Adventures* are typical of the variations on the theme of the black woman. To cast pearls before swine is a provocative idea and perhaps lies as a submerged thought in my naming of these characters.

A *diffy* in the black idiom is a streetwalker. A *sediddy* is one who is overly sedate; a *peola,* a light-skinned black woman; *Aunt Jane,* a female Uncle Tom. A *band* is a woman, a *banana* is also a light-skinned female. A *Banta issue* is a pretty black girl. A young woman is also a *bantam,* and so on. But the most common names are Hagi, Jane, and peola, terms still in use.

The lore and literature, the myth and conjecture, and the factual history of the past are at all times present in me. I write from the black experience for an audience as free and as large as I can find. I write from a love of creating and fabricating. I write in disguise in search of truth. I develop black folktales from the Plantation Era as a metaphor for present-day struggles and accomplishments of American blacks. These folktales demonstrate that tale-telling is not merely a thing of the past, but a continuing cultural imperative.

I see black literature and the literature I create as a social action. Black people are an oppressed people. There is little black writing that is not socially conscious and race-conscious writing. There is no other way but this way for a black writer to be considered a writer of truth in this society. The very substance of our thinking is of struggle, becoming, and change. There is thesis and antithesis in search of synthesis. All of my young characters live within a fictional social order, and it is largely a black social order that is characterized by tension, insecurity, and struggle. The final analysis is one of growing consciousness. That is what history teaches us, or should.

I believe in the preservation of life and literature, the documentary history of the struggle in schools, in colleges and libraries for coming generations of Americans. Imaginative use of language and ideas illuminates for us a human condition, and we are reminded again to care who we Americans are. In this instance, who are these black people, where do they come from, how do they dream, how do they hunger? And we are reminded to value what we have and to know always what we want.

I am pleased to have this opportunity to share some of my reasons for being and my words with you.

Thank you.

NOTES

1. Virginia Hamilton, *The People Could Fly: American Black Folktales* (New York: Knopf, 1985), pp. 61–62.
2. William L. Van Deburg, *The Slave Drivers: Black Agricultural Labor Supervisors in the Antebellum South,* (Westport, CT: Greenwood Press, 1979), p. 14.
3. John Langston Gwaltney, *Drylongso* (New York: Random House, 1981).

Introduction to Robert Cormier

ROBERT CORMIER'S BOOKS signal an ever-growing interest in children's and young adult literature as comprising some of the most challenging books published today. They offer, not a hopeful confirmation that everything's possible through the wisdom of mature adjustment, but a confrontation with situations that test and defeat the human spirit because they seem impossible. Most children's and young adult books have followed a folkloric tradition that J. R. R. Tolkien labels "Eucatastrophe," the happy climax to a potentially tragic situation. There may be violence done and nasty villains — in fact, both are present in imaginative abundance throughout oral literature, much of which is amoral. But for the hero or heroine, things ultimately turn out all right. While Cormier's books do have some mythical aspects, however, they often detail the triumphant machinations of evil.

Like adults, children are both repelled and fascinated by evil. Preschool children are magnetized by fairy tale forces of good and evil that symbolize elements in their own world. Eight- and nine-year-olds carve swastikas on school desks and evince interest in a dictator whose historical context is completely beyond their knowledge. Teenagers still clamor for Mick Jagger's "Sympathy for the Devil" because it expresses something powerful within and beyond their experience. Young adults are drawn to Robert Cormier's novels, at least partly, because he explores the nature of evil in society and its source, the individual.

Following the publication of several adult novels and short stories, Cormier's first young adult book, *The Chocolate War,* electrified readers in 1974 and became a landmark in the development of YA literature. Since then, he has published four other novels, each singular but all intense in probing the depths of a tragic situation. At the conclusion of *Beyond the Chocolate War,* the arch-villain, Archie, says to a follower berating him for his cruelty, "You could have said *no* anytime, anytime at all . . . you had free choice, buddy." And later, ". . . I'm all the things you hide inside you." Archie, Brother Leon, and their cronies function as evil incarnate, but beyond the archetypal characters at Trinity High School, Cormier has delved, through other books, into the complexities of balance between good and evil in each human being. Like Tolkien's poignant villain, Gollum, the terrorist in *After the First Death* has the capacity for kindness before his fall from grace. Moreover, his decision for evil is shaped by the evil that has been done him as part of his own past. Political villainy, whether overt or secret, crushes the individual physically and spiritually. Against devastating social evils that can overwhelm and victimize them, young people react sometimes by destroying society, and sometimes by destroying themselves.

Supporting the thematic substance of Cormier's work is an implacable sense of plot and an increasingly sophisticated narrative voice, in which witnesses may or may not be reliable, according to the way each reader interprets ambiguities of event and conclusion. I quail to think of how Mr. Cormier's feature columns read during his many years of reporting for *The Fitchburg Sentinel* in Massachusetts. The mild-mannered man you see before you is a devilish schemer when it comes to pacing a story. In fact, he is distinguished not only for a best-seller status in the relatively new field of young adult literature, but also for being the subject of a study guide, a sure indication of his critical importance. His books have consistently been selected by American Library Association committees for their annual lists of Best Books for Young Adults. If you have not read Cormier's novels, prepare for a gripping, unnerving experience. They do not end happily, but they offer readers the chance to consider choices that Cormier's fictional characters do not have. If you have read Robert Cormier's books, you will be intrigued by this opportunity to hear him speak. Mr. Cormier.

Robert Cormier

I, Too, Am the Cheese
May 8, 1987

ON TUESDAY AFTERNOON this week, the telephone rang at my home in Massachusetts. A young voice said, "This is Amy. Is that you, Dad?" I said, "Yes, it is."

I think most of you know why I said yes. It's generally known that the telephone number that Adam, in *I Am the Cheese,* uses to call his girlfriend, Amy, is my own phone number. And I get at least a call a day, have since the book was published. So naturally, when this girl calling herself Amy asked if I was her dad, I said yes. Automatically. I've been playing that role for years.

Then I said, "What's the matter?"

And she said, "They're holding me prisoner here."

I said, "Is Adam with you?"

She said, "Yes."

I said, "Where are you being held?"

There was a pause on the line, I heard muffled voices.

Then she came on again and said, "In Burlington."

I should add here that I had spoken last week at the Champlain Valley Union High School in Burlington, Vermont.

"Can you help me?" she asked.

I said, "Wait a minute," and lifted the telephone into the air.

It so happens that we are having renovations done at our house, converting our garage into a family room. This seems like a ridiculous thing to do, since our children are all grown and away from home. But your children go away one by one and manage to return two by two and three by three.

Anyway, I held the phone up so that Amy could hear the hammers pounding away and a buzz saw sawing away.

"Hear that?" I asked.

"Yes," she said.

"Well," I said. "I'm afraid I can't help you, Amy. I'm being held prisoner, too. In fact, they're boarding me in right this minute to make sure I don't escape."

"That's too bad," she said.

"Know what we should do?"

"What?" she asked.

"Write another novel. . . ."

That's one of the things that happened this week to a writer whose novels have brought him the title of Young Adult Author.

Here's another thing that happened:

Another phone call. This time, Monday. A call from Zena Sutherland. She called at a time when I was thinking about the talk I would be giving later in the week — tonight in fact — in her honor.

Seems she was checking the time my plane would arrive at Midway Airport, since she was picking me up. She had the right time, but the wrong airline. We straightened it out. And then she did a thing that made me glad I'm here tonight, and proves what a great lady she is and how irresistible. Suddenly, over the phone she sang, "I'll be down to get you in a taxi, honey." Who could resist a woman like that?

When *Beyond the Chocolate War,* the sequel to my 1974 novel *The Chocolate War,* was published in 1985, my publishers ran a series of advertisements announcing the new book. Included in the copy were words that ran to the effect that *The Chocolate War* had been published all those years ago to unanimous acclaim. This may seem so in retrospect, but this was certainly not the case. Almost immediately, the book met with disapproval. I had not realized in writing the novel that I had smashed some taboos — I had not realized this because I had not been aware of writing a book that would be marketed as a young adult novel. I think all of this is pretty well known now, certainly by those assembled here tonight. But the reason why I am telling this story is that *The Chocolate War* might very well have gone into oblivion almost at the moment of being published because of those early reviews, certainly some in advance of publication. Like *Publishers Weekly,* for instance, which criticized the novel for its supposedly anti-Catholic bias, claiming the writer had allowed his bitterness against the church to spoil his novel. Yet, the novel did not die, and in fact, met with great success because certain people came to its rescue and defense. I was unaware of the battle going on at the time. I knew nothing of the YA world, the editors, and critics. I realize now, of course, how much that novel was at risk and how many traditions it did demolish. That it succeeded was due to the efforts of a certain few people who believed in it, who saw what others did not see, or did not see what others thought they saw.

Among these people was Zena Sutherland.

Thank goodness for people like her, Marilyn Marlow,

my agent, Patricia Campbell, and, of course, Fabio Coen, my editor at Pantheon, who published the book and did not worry about language or the downbeat ending.

As I became familiar with the YA world, became a part of it, in fact, I realized that Zena's championing went far beyond one book; it pervaded the entire genre. The world of children's literature might have been very different if not for her presence in it, and her influence. Besides all this, who can resist the lady who sang, "Be down to get you in a taxi, honey" and actually picked me up in a limousine.

Because of Zena Sutherland, I am doing some things tonight I never did before. I am reading this speech. I actually wrote down this speech and can hardly believe that I did such a thing. Usually I wing it. The speech was written roughly, with a lot of crossing-outs, single-space, because I am a terrible typist. I type my novels on an old green Royal manual office machine, without any electricity or electronics involved. Actually, I would not be doing this if the committee in charge of this event hadn't said that they would like a written speech so that it could be reproduced later. I am not sure they will want to reproduce this, but figured I would write it anyway, to keep my end of the bargain. My wife, Connie, who does the final typing of my manuscripts, will type this one, too, if the committee is still interested. What Zena Sutherland has also made me do tonight is talk about things I have never talked about before to an audience. Maybe to friends sitting around at night. Bits and pieces to people now and then across the years. I want to talk about a writer by the name of Robert Cormier who wrote other things besides the young adult novels that bear his name. And I'd like to trace that person to the person you see before you at this moment, who would not be here if it were not for these other writings.

I am known to most people as the author of *The Chocolate War* and other YA books.

But I have through the years written three other novels — *Now and at the Hour; A Little Raw on Monday Mornings;* and *Take Me Where the Good Times Are* — plus from seventy-five to one hundred stories which appeared in magazines or weren't published at all. (*Unpublished*, of course, is a euphemism for *rejected*.) I also for ten years wrote a human-interest column for my hometown newspaper, *The Fitchburg Sentinel*.

There is no violence in these books and stories and columns. There is also —

Ah, but let me be specific. I want to tell you about the first story of mine that was published — and the first novel — and one of the columns that reflects me as a young man and also as a man not so young.

I have always believed that a writer is allowed one coincidence in a book. More than one is fatal, but one is acceptable. And there is one coincidence involved in this talk tonight — the fact that I am speaking here in the month of May.

This has been a special month for me for twenty-eight years. My father, whom I loved with a love that has never diminished, died on May 22, 1959. He died in my arms at ten minutes after six in the morning, after suffering for many months. He was my father and my friend. We were buddies. We weren't the type who went fishing together, and we were not involved in Little League. I would have disgraced him as a ball player, anyway. We shared the agony of being Red Sox fans and thus had our hearts broken every September when we sat at the old Emerson radio in the kitchen. My father was a very great man, although he did not know this. He worked in a factory all his life, at a bench. He brought up seven children and mourned forever the eighth child who died at the age of three. He kissed my mother whenever he left the house and whenever he came in the door. He smoked Chesterfield cigarettes. One of the great comforts of my life was my father smoking. Someone would wake up from a bad dream at night and my father would be there. I remember a terrible time of my life when I had nightmares after my tonsils were removed at the hospital. My father would say, "Go to sleep. I'll be up a while. I'm going to have a cigarette." What a comfort. Because to me, in those days a cigarette seemed to last forever. And knowing that my father was sitting up, in the middle of the night, in the old chair by the window, smoking, on guard, let me drift off into sweet sleep. I knew that my father loved me. That he would die for me. That if fire swept the house, he would rescue me. That he would not let anything terrible happen to me.

I said we were buddies, and we were. When television first arrived, people watched in the bars or in the windows of furniture stores. Milton Berle on Tuesday nights. Or they gathered at the home of the richer relatives to watch the events on that glowing tube. My father and I watched the Red Sox on television at the Welcome Bar, where everybody was welcome. I was a young man then, newly married, and my wife, Connie, would visit with my mother while my father and I went to the neighborhood bar and sipped beer as the Red Sox lost again, even though they boasted Ted Williams and Bobby Doer and Rudy York. And in the shadows of the late afternoon, mellowed by the beer, we made our way home through the streets of French Hill, arms around each other, father and son, but most of all, friends and buddies as we relived the game, secure in our love and friendship and brotherhood. And Connie saw us weaving down the street and told me later that, yes, we were late for supper and obviously had had a bit too much to drink, but we both looked so happy together. That was a beautiful moment for me.

And so it's May again, and spikes of forsythia brighten what has been a gloomy spring of rain and snow in New England. And the twenty-second of the month approaches again. And I remembered my father as I wrote these words I would be speaking later. Ironically, the cigarettes that he smoked all those years, as he toiled away at the factory and in the middle of the night to bring his children comfort — those same cigarettes probably killed him. He died of lung cancer. It haunts me that I am older now than the age my father was when he died. His death left me more than sorrow and sadness and regret. It left me searing, soaring with anger. And as always, when emotions sweep me, I go to the typewriter. I wrote dried-eyed, burned-out, about how it is for a man to die. And as I wrote I had a strange feeling about what I was doing. I didn't know whether anybody would ever read what I was writing — I considered it therapy — but in the writing I wanted to put everyone who would ever read it in bed with my father, and make them die a little too.

That was my first novel, *Now and at the Hour*, published fourteen years before *The Chocolate War*. But I would not have been able to write *The Chocolate War* if not for that first novel.

The first story of mine to be published was titled "The Little Things That Count." I have spoken before of how

Miss Florence Conlon, a teacher at Fitchburg State College, sold this story for me. She showed interest in my writing and said she'd like to see one of my stories sometime. I was delighted to have an audience besides my mother, who had been my only reader up to that time. I wrote the story on the kitchen table at home, pen and paper, and brought it to Miss Conlon, who kept it awhile, had it typed without my knowledge, and arrived at my house a few weeks later with a seventy-five-dollar check. She had sold it to *The Sign,* a national Catholic magazine which is still being published. That's pretty well known, at least to people who have heard me speak or have read an article about me.

But I'd like to share a bit more about that story with you tonight, and to trace some roots. Those roots have to do with my mother. She was my first reader after Sister Catherine discovered me at St. Cecilia's Parochial School in the seventh grade and declared that I was a writer. But I think that my mother was more of an influence on me beyond my writing, that unconsciously she helped me discover the essence of storytelling.

You see, my mother is now eighty-six and in vigorous health, although the tragedy of her life is that her eyes are bad and she cannot read any longer the books she loves. She is a woman of promises. She has always kept her promises to me. And she has kept her promises to God.

My mother gave birth to eight children. In those early years of her marriage, she was in frail health. She was finally struck by an illness that was life-threatening. She envisioned her small children left motherless and, in her pain and panic, made a bargain with God. If He would allow her to live and bring up her children, she promised two things: First, she would wear blue and white for the rest of her life — these were the colors of the Holy Virgin Mary, the Mother of God, to whom she had a special devotion. Her second promise: She would never go to the movies again. She who loved movies — she who also loved to wear bright and vivid colors.

I, too, have always loved the movies. Books and movies. I sometimes think movies had the greatest influence on me as a writer, because the movies of my youth — those golden years of the thirties and forties — told wonderful stories. And because my mother did not, could not, go to the movies, I brought them to her. I'd come home from those Saturday or Sunday matinees at the Plymouth or the Met and tell her scene by scene what happened — Bette Davis in *Dark Victory*, Merle Oberon in *'Til We Meet Again*, James Cagney in *City for Conquest*, and John Garfield, most of all, with the Lane sisters in *Four Daughters*. I think I learned my sense of story, pacing, and characterization as I told my mother those movie stories, scene by scene, taking all the parts, watching her respond to the tales. Perhaps I subconsciously absorbed the way drama develops. Whenever I write, I don't think in terms of chapters, but in scenes. Anyway, my mother listened. She was probably bored when I recited the story of some action hit like Errol Flynn in *Captain Blood* or the plots of a hundred "B" movies. But she listened.

She still wears blue and white. You can't imagine the various shades of blue she has worn throughout those years. We have tried to slip some green into her fashions on occasion, calling it "teal blue." But the eyes that are not sharp enough to read anymore are sharp enough to know when the dress or the sweater is not really blue or white.

When I was eleven years old, my mother was taken suddenly ill on a Sunday afternoon when I was alone with her. I did not realize she was having a miscarriage. It was the fall of the year. I remember that, because my father was at a political rally, listening to candidates making speeches. She dispatched me to bring my father home, gasping through her pain and trying to disguise it from me. I brought my father home to her and he took charge, somehow summoning the doctor — we had no telephone. I went to church, St. Cecilia's Church, a stone's-throw away from our house — knelt at the altar rail, desperate, having seen my mother in the nakedness of her pain. And following her example, I offered up a promise to God. I would wear blue for the rest of my life. I knew the impossibility of this promise even as I made it. This was the Depression. We wore hand-me-downs; I knew I could have no control over what I wore. Ah, but I knew what I could control. I then promised God to wear a blue necktie, and no other color of necktie for the rest of my life. We wore neckties to school every day. I knew that I could manage that.

My mother recovered, blossomed, full of life again, and I began to wear a blue necktie. One of my own, and then one borrowed from my brother. I don't remember all the details of my subterfuge and my maneuvers to avoid the neckties that were any other color but blue. I remember that it was a desperate game I played. I remember wearing one necktie until it curled as if in protest. There were not that many blue neckties in the house. I sneaked into my parent's bedroom and borrowed one of my father's. Too big, but I wore it anyway. My brother Norman — he and I slept together from the time we were little kids until the night before I was married — became suspicious first. But then, he always thought I was strange anyway, preferring books to baseball.

Finally, my mother noticed what was going on. Mothers always find out eventually. And I confessed what happened. She explained to me that promises made under duress and strain had no power to bind. But what about her and her promises? Somehow, she explained it away to me. I can't remember her exact words. To me, she was so beautiful and lovely and sweet and honest that whatever she told me I took as gospel truth. Somehow, she convinced me that she could wear blue and white forever and not go to the movies, but that God would never ask an eleven-year-old boy to wear a blue necktie for the rest of his life.

At the age of nineteen, one of the key episodes in the first short story of mine to be published was about a boy whose mother was very sick and the boy promised to wear a blue necktie for the rest of his life . . . and his mother told him he didn't have to.

So even then, the events of my life, the emotions that stormed my days and nights, furnished the stuff of my stories. The seeds of the stories in *Eight Plus One* were planted in those first tentative stories I wrote on the kitchen table, at the corner of Fifth and Water Streets on French Hill in Leominster, Massachusetts — surrounded by my mother and father and my brothers and sisters.

Many people have read those earlier novels of mine, including the novel based on my father's death, and many have also read that first short story and the stories in *Eight Plus One*, but few people outside of my hometown area have read the human-interest columns I wrote for *The Fitchburg Sentinel* and earlier, the *Worcester Telegram* — a thousand of them, give or take a few. The Fitchburg

columns were written under the pseudonym of John Fitch
IV — in honor of a man by the name of John Fitch, who
founded the city of Fitchburg. I chose a pseudonym because I knew this would be a very personal human-interest
column and I did not want to invade the privacy of the
people I knew and loved. The columns cover a wide range
— seeking the small shocks of recognition, family columns, movie and book reviews, observations of life in a
small New England City, nostalgia. Nostalgia is a city I
visit often, although I would not want to live there.

I'd like tonight to share one of those columns with you.
It's not the best column and not the worst. When you
write a regular column, you know your reach won't always exceed your grasp. I chose this column because —
I'm not sure. All of my manuscripts and stories and unpublished works, letters, reviews, critical articles, stories I
wrote, editorials, and feature stories are collected at Fitchburg State College. And I went up there this week to look
over the columns to find a suitable one or two for this talk.
I picked this one and it was serendipity. It's called: "God,
How I Loved That Suit." I didn't know at the time that I
would also be telling you tonight about the boy with the
blue necktie. Let me read this column to you.

> God, how I loved that suit. It was blue. And it was
> double-breasted, with a pinstripe. It was the first
> thing I'd ever bought on a charge account. I must
> have been, oh, 18 or 19, and working for the first
> time in a big city.
>
> When I tried the suit on in the store, I immediately
> stood straighter and taller and I felt like Cary Grant
> or, maybe, William Powell. I know that dates me,

but what the hell. The tailor came over, the measuring tape draped around his collar, and he made chalkmarks here and there but said the suit didn't really need much tailoring, it just had to be taken in a little.

I remember taking it home and putting it on in the bedroom, posing for a while before the bureau mirror and tilting the mirror so that I could get a full-length view. Then I strolled into the living room, carefully casual.

My mother looked up and said the kind of things mothers always say. "It's just beautiful," she said. "Handsome."

I can't remember now where I wore the suit for the first time. Maybe a dance at Whalom Park ballroom on a Monday night in the time when people like Duke Ellington and Vaughn Monroe played there.

But I can remember the way I felt when I walked up the street, the way my shoulders swung, the feeling that every eye was upon me and that I was God's gift to mankind, if only for the moment.

* * *

I think of all this now because I came across an old family picture album the other day. It was a rainy afternoon and I was cleaning some shelves. I opened the album and there before me on the page was the yellowed photograph.

It was a family picture, the kind people take on special Sundays and holidays. We were grouped on the front lawn and you can see part of the front porch. It looked like all the family photographs ever taken: somebody squinting into the sun and someone else not looking at the camera.

My mother is in the picture. She's smiling, a smile

tinged with pride, and I guess it is pride in the children standing with her. In the picture, she is forever young, and it struck me as I studied the photo how she hasn't really changed through the years. Older, of course, as we all are. But her eyes still innocent and the sweetness still in her face.

My father is not in the picture because he was taking it. One hand sheltering the light so that he could see us reflected in the little rectangular opening. And then he'd say the usual funny things, trying to make us all smile. And we'd tell him to hurry up. It's hard for kids to stand still for more than 10 seconds or so.

He wasn't the greatest photographer in the world. He'd always pose us looking into the sun and in some of the pictures you can see his shadow. He's dead now. But in many ways, his shadow is still with us, a sweet presence in our lives.

* * *

It's impossible to stop once you start looking at the pictures in an old album like that. That past sweeps over you in waves and the emotions are many and varied. The rain outside is like a curtain sealing you off from the present.

I look at a picture of my brother in uniform. He is posed before the window on the front of the house and a star is hanging in the window, signifying that our family had a serviceman in the war. His garrison hat — I think that's what they called them: the one with the visor — is pushed back on his head in that casual way the fellows wore them on furlough. Or while their pictures were being taken. I remember the excitement when he'd arrive home on a three-day pass, weary, much-traveled, and how we'd gather

round him, the younger kids in awe of their uni-
formed brother.　　*　*　*

I look at photographs of my sisters and marvel at
how beautiful they were. In those days, I thought of
them only as my sisters and sisters were simply that
— not beautiful and not ugly, either. But now I see
that they were really good-looking and no wonder
the phone rang in the evenings and the cars pulled
into the driveway.

There's also the picture of a child long dead, a
golden-haired child, dead at three years old. His
memory is a faint blur to me. I was five at the time.
My mother said that I always took good care of him
when we played outdoors. But I don't remember, of
course. I wish I did. It would make a nice memory to
have.　　*　*　*

And so I leafed through the album and it was sad
and nostalgic. I returned to that first picture, the one
in which I was wearing that new pin-striped suit.

The fellow in the picture was me, all right, but also
a complete stranger. He was the same height but he
looked, I don't know, vulnerable, unguarded, viola-
ble. Was I ever really that innocent, I wondered.

And the suit. Shoulders too broad. The pinstripe
made the suit look a bit ridiculous, the kind the gang-
sters wore in those old Warner Brothers movies. I
saw that I wasn't the dashing figure I had thought
myself and that the suit had failed to transform me
into Cary Grant, after all.

I closed the album and sat there awhile. I guess
looking at old photographs is not the best thing in
the world to do on a rainy afternoon.[1]

And maybe telling you all this is not the best thing to be doing on a Friday night in Chicago in honor of Zena Sutherland. But I always give in to my emotions. I knew this would be a special evening, a celebration, that I would be following such wonderful writers and human beings as Maurice Sendak and Lloyd Alexander and Katherine Paterson and Virginia Hamilton. Talk about being intimidated, especially for someone who does not write speeches but merely likes to talk and ramble a bit, with no great messages to impart. So I thought I would share with you some of the moments that contributed to the man not many of you know if you only know the man who wrote *The Chocolate War* or who has been interviewed about his adult life as husband and father and, these days, grandfather. I wanted to tell you about the boy — after all, the boy is father to the man — the boy who promised to wear a blue necktie for the rest of his life, who recited movies to his mother, and who drank beer and watched ball games with his father, the young man who wore that pin-striped suit.

In many ways, I am still that boy with the blue necktie — and if I did not keep that promise to God, there are other promises that I tried to keep.

My great good thanks for allowing me to be a part of this celebration for Zena Sutherland.

NOTE

1. "God, How I Loved That Suit," *Fitchburg Sentinel,* July 26, 1973.

Introduction to Paula Fox

REVIEWING PAULA FOX'S NOVELS, which I have had the privilege of doing several times in the past twenty years, is a frustrating as well as pleasurable experience. One observation leads to another, until the reviewer has gone well beyond the limits of space generally allotted for reviews, and still barely brushed the surface of the story. A Paula Fox novel demands and sustains the most expansive mode of criticism. Although her crafting is distinguished by a singular internal clarity, it also has a depth of imagery that reaches a reader deep into the core of the characters. I once heard her say, in fact, that her approach to characterizations resembled peeling an onion, getting closer and closer to the center.

That is true of both her adult and her children's books. An action exists to reveal the actors in their complexity, yet not a word appears that doesn't need to be there. To balance the needs of nuance and clarity is no mean feat. The most recent examples include four books — *One-Eyed Cat; The Moonlight Man; Lily and the Lost Boy;* and *The Village by the Sea.* Each is distinguished, as are all Fox's children's books, by unforgettable portraits of a young protagonist facing some strategic choice of maturation, and an adult who has made those choices, for better or for worse. The plots, of course, are completely different. In *One-Eyed Cat,* a boy purges his guilt over blinding an animal with the first proud shot of his rifle. In *The Moonlight Man,* a girl demythifies her alcoholic father. *Lily and the Lost Boy* reenacts a Greek tragedy of sacrifice and redemption.

The Village by the Sea is an intensive portrait of three characters that reverberates with insights emerging from a child's involvement with her game. Emma must stay with her aunt and uncle while her father has heart surgery and her mother attends him. Adding to her concern about her father is the stress of hostile remarks from Aunt Bea, an ex-alcoholic who is obsessed by old family jealousies: ". . . she has a habit of resentment. It's a kind of addiction, too, like brandy." This grip of hatred causes Aunt Bea to destroy the miniature village which Emma and a friend have spent weeks creating from flotsam they find on the shore. Bea's fury seems contagious, and Emma barely overcomes, with the help of her uncle, a violent urge for vengeance in the larger context of the adults' village by the sea. More than ever, Fox's style is compressed without seeming dense, each scene and image allowed space for clean effect. Although the development is sophisticated, the viewpoint is unfalteringly that of the child. The novel is easy to read and complex to consider, an encounter that moves the reader from Gothic narrative suspense to compassionate illumination of the dark in human nature.

The children in these books do not emerge unscarred from their encounters, but they and their readers are stronger for the echoes of understanding that reflect off the incident. Part of the reason for this is that Fox creates a kind of echo chamber with her prose. It is hard, clear, compact, and smooth, with thoughts further refined as they bounce from point to point. Zena Sutherland has called her the greatest stylist of children's literature. Above all, there is the patience of credible development. Nothing is told that can be shown, with the result that each reader discovers a truth of his or her own rather than of the writer's prescription. That is a rare achievement in any book, but especially in the context of the traditional didacticism that too often marks juvenile fiction.

Even in a book as politically charged as *The Slave Dancer,* which won the Newbery medal in 1972, Fox allows the situation to speak for itself. This has roused great controversy, for the narrative is a young fifer's report of a voyage aboard a slave ship, and some would prefer a diatribe. Yet the tragic ironies of injustice are as clear to children as they are to adults. I quote from a twelve-year-old's essay:

> The way Paula Fox writes this book is to pick out small, insignificant people and show their misery, because those are the people who make up the majority of slaves. She took a small white boy, and without any blood and gore, showed him some of the most horrible things in the world.
>
> She also showed a lot of human nature. Purvis, for example, was the best man on the whole ship, but he put on a pretense of being a rough sailor. Ben Stout, on the other hand, acts kind and gentle, but is really a nasty cruel person. There are bad men, and there are bad men.

Trust in the power of the craft and the perception of the reader characterizes the best writers in any genre. That

Fox brings this respect to nine-year-olds as well as ninety-year-olds is rare indeed. A good children's book provides privacy for free thought, for reflection on the human condition and its moral implications. That is not to say that Fox's work is without its moments of gripping tension. One reviewer said of a 1967 book, *How Many Miles to Babylon,* that "the suspense devices are worthy of Hitchcock." Most important, however, Fox projects the imaginative life of children not as fey or droll but as intense and all-powerful.

Paula Fox has been widely recognized for her sixteen children's and six adult books. Since *Maurice's Room* was published in 1966, she has been the recipient of a Guggenheim Fellowship and an American Academy Award (1972); the American Library Association Newbery Medal and the National Endowment for the Arts Award (1974); and the Hans Christian Andersen International Medal for the entire body of her work (1978). *One-Eyed Cat* was a Newbery Honor Book in 1985.

It is with great pleasure and anticipation that I introduce our sixth Sutherland lecturer, Paula Fox.

Paula Fox

Unquestioned Answers
May 6, 1988

IN A CHECK-OUT LINE at the market, a young woman in front of me exclaimed to a companion, "Oh! It's like raining." What is it, one might wonder, that is like raining? But whatever was falling against the plate glass didn't resemble rain. It *was* rain.

Like has broken loose from hip talk, once its province, and taken root in the daily language of observation and emotion, often as involuntary as a tic. "It's like sad," said a boy of the shooting death of a classmate in a gang-beleaguered school in Brooklyn. There's a significant shade of difference between *rain* and *like rain;* between *sad* and *like sad.* Meaningless, without a grammatical function, *like* in these two sentences serves to postpone for a second or two the realization of rain and death.

To say, "It is raining"; to say, "I feel sad," is concrete. But as George Orwell wrote in 1949, the "whole tendency of modern prose is away from concreteness." To illustrate his statement, he wrote a parody of a verse from Ecclesiastes. Here is the verse: "I returned, and saw under the sun that the race is not with the swift, nor the battle to the strong, neither yet bread to the wise, nor yet riches to men of understanding, nor yet favor to men of skill; but time and chance happeneth to them all."

And here is Orwell's transformation of it: "Objective consideration of contemporary phenomena compels the conclusion that success or failure in competitive activities exhibits no tendency to be commensurate with innate capacity, but that a considerable element of the unpredictable must invariably be taken into account."

When we hear that the youngest sibling in a family unit, encouraged by his role models, has begun to communicate interpersonally, do we gain more knowledge than if we are told that a baby has begun to talk with his mother and father?

I hope you will bear with me while I read a few scraps from an evaluation of a book I wrote called *The Moonlight Man*. My intention is to illustrate the murder of language, and therefore of meaning, not to complain about an unsympathetic response. The reviewer writes:

> The father . . . is an alcoholic and an interesting, but fairly unproductive person . . . the daughter acts as a facilitator for his alcoholism which is not a healthy role model for students who may face this problem. The book is about her separation from her parents as individuals, but it closes with her father abandoning her. The task of final separation from parents does not belong to junior high students and I do not think this age needs to face parental abandonment. Furthermore, if a child is dealing with an alcoholic parent, this book does not give acceptable guidance to work on that problem.

I believe this report to contain a basic perversion of what literature and stories are concerned with — the condition of being human. It is written in the jargon of social science. The writer does not like the book and is unable to say so. Instead, she evokes a contemporary vision of virtue and sin: productivity and unproductivity. The father should be the daughter's client — or patient. The story is not acceptable because it does not give "guidance."

What I am concerned with here is the deadening of language, an extreme form of alienation expressed in words that have no resonance, and absolutely no inner reference to living people. "This age does not need to face parental abandonment," the reviewer writes. Leaving aside the question of whether or not abandonment is involved, what on earth is "this age"? Who need not face what? Which boys? Which girls? What human beings?

It appears to be a tendency of some social disciplines to become intellectually petrified and spiritually lifeless if an opposing impulse does not come into play.

The most cursory glance at changes in thinking about human psychology over the last fifty years suggests we can only hypothesize about the meaning of behavior. New information is always arriving; the last word is never in.

Partly, perhaps, because we do not have the steadying forms of older cultures to fall back on, we are, in this country, more open to new ideas. But we are also, it seems to me, more inclined to hail the new as absolute truth — until the next *new* comes along.

Nietzsche said, "Everything absolute leads to pathology." A physicist of our own day, Dr. David Bohm, writes that "most categories are so familiar to us that they are used almost unconsciously . . . it is possible for categories to become so fixed a part of the intellect that the mind finally becomes engaged in playing false to support them."

There is another consequence of the fossilization of intellect that is both cause and result of a dependence on categories, on everything absolute, on labels. I touched upon it in speaking of the use of *like* to postpone realization. Labels not only free us from the obligation to think creatively; they numb our sensibilities, our power to feel. During the Vietnam War, the phrase *body count* entered our vocabulary. It is an ambiguous phrase, inorganic, even faintly sporty. It distanced us from the painful reality of corpses, of dead, mutilated people.

The language of labels is like paper money, issued irresponsibly, with nothing of intrinsic value behind it, that is, with no effort of the intelligence to see, to really apprehend.

George Orwell wrote that if thought corrupts language, language can also corrupt thought. An example of that is racial expletives which, once used, eat away at the capacity of the imagination to grasp the reality of other human beings, what George Eliot described in her novel *Middlemarch* as "the deep-seated habit of direct fellow feeling with individual fellow men."

In a terrible event in Queens, New York, several years ago, white teenagers howled racial expletives as they drove one black man to his death and then savagely beat another. What is to become of us all without fellow feeling? How are we to develop it in children if we do not feel it toward them? If we treat them as a race apart, substituting management techniques and hollow classifications for the sympathy and companionship we all long for in the life we share?

Children do not have judgment; they have not lived long enough for that, or for the detachment that is part of judgment. Because of that, they need the protection of adults. But in nearly every other sense, they are simply ourselves when new.

When I was a child, people used to say, "These are the best years of your life. Just wait till you grow up!" My childhood was painful — if these were the best days, I wondered, what on earth was coming next? As I grew older, I learned that people, often born in less obviously difficult circumstances than my own, had suffered disappointment, pain, bafflement, just as I had. The years of childhood are not necessarily the best or the worst, they are the first years of our lives. When we forget that, we forget our mutual humanity, and in so doing, strip children of their dignity and mysteries.

A radio interviewer, in connection with the book of mine that I mentioned earlier, having asserted that he was an optimist, asked me why my story didn't have a more upbeat ending. People like happy endings, he said, in the vaguely threatening voice I have come to expect from optimists. "Some people don't," was all I could manage to reply. What he wanted, I felt, was untruth, a Disneyfication of story, blandness, looking on the bright side, because that is what is supposed to be good for children. He seemed indifferent to an ending that might be true to the story that preceded it.

We are not the only people in the world who like happy tragedies. From the end of the seventeenth century to 1834, *King Lear* was given a happy ending. Cordelia didn't die.

It is not fitting that children be burdened, in service to some transcendent idea of truth, with the knowledge of all the failures of human society and of individual lives, which in any case they can't assimilate. But there are so many children who have experienced those failures in their flesh and bones, in their spirits! Yet, they are creatures of hope, even in the direst circumstances — and they need hope.

"My mother groan'd! my father wept. / Into the dangerous world I leapt . . ." wrote the poet, William Blake. Don't we sense in our very cells that it is a dangerous world? And isn't it because of that deep presentiment, that we can become brave?

I want to tell you about some of the brave children I have known.

Soon after the end of World War II, I was for a year a string reporter — the lowest rung in journalism — for an English wire service. One of the places I visited was a former vacation estate of a Prussian aristocrat in the Tatra mountains on the Polish-Czechoslovak border. The Polish government had converted it into a kind of recovery residence for children who had been born in concentration camps, or who had spent part of their childhood in them. Without exception, their parents had been murdered by the Nazis.

Our small group of reporters arrived one mid-afternoon after a lengthy, bone-chilling drive through the winter-silent landscape. It was not yet dark. There were twelve or thirteen boys and girls, and a small staff, in the grand, bleak house, its walls bare, its floors stripped of rugs and recovered with linoleum, its vast uncovered windows white with the glare from the snow-covered mountains.

It was impossible to tell the ages of the children, they were so stunted. They were very glad to see us, and they clung to us, grasping our hands as they showed us their classroom; then a former salon now filled with narrow, neatly made-up cots; a library long emptied of books, its shelves containing a few toys and games; and the dining room, where we ate an early supper with them at a long trestle table covered with yellow oilcloth.

After supper, a woman from Dublin who was among our group and who sang wonderfully, gave the children a concert. They sat with rapt attention as she sang in her sweet soprano of the Molly Maguires, of massacres and betrayals, and Irish boys with bullets in their breasts fallen on the moors.

A Yugoslav and two Czech journalists spoke Polish. The rest of us depended on an interpreter. The children wanted to know where we had come from and why, did we live in houses, and what were they like? And if we had children — where were they, with us so far away? They did not speak of their own histories except in the most indirect way, and then, not in words. They were painfully alert to any sudden movement on our part; they fell into abrupt silence in the midst of merriment when they seemed to sink into a dream, and they would suddenly burst into laughter that was almost frantic.

A boy whose English name would have been Richard asked me through the interpreter to call him that. He didn't want his Polish name. He asked me to go with him to one of the huge gardens that surrounded the mansion. I thought he was nine or so. I was told he was fourteen.

We went through the French doors of the dining room. It was nearly dark now. He held my hand as we walked along a partly cleared path, snow-laden shrubbery leaning toward us, the bare branches of winter-blackened trees above us. It was a somber, frozen, lonely place, the heart of winter. He ran a few feet ahead of me, and with his arms and hands, brushed the snow from what I thought was a column which might have once supported some heroic or mythological statue. It was a large birdbath.

He smiled at me and pointed to the sky. He made flying motions with his arms, then fluttered his hands more and more slowly as the wings of the bird he was imitating closed around its body, and it landed on the rim of the birdbath. He turned his head at an angle, then stretched forward as though to drink. His hands fluttered once again, his arms waved, the bird flew away. He shook snow from a bush, motioned me to look closely, pointed to a twig, put his hands together beneath his chin, then gradually widened them. I kicked away some snow from the ground. The earth looked like iron. I bent down and pretended my arm was a stalk that was growing up through the soil. I opened my fingers to sniff the petals of an imaginary flower. He let out a small shout of laughter and grabbed my hand and pressed it against his head. I had understood he was describing the coming of spring.

Before we left that evening, the children sang to us. Their pale faces were flushed with the pleasure of giving us their song. When we left, they crowded around the great entrance. They wept. But they stood quietly as we backed down the cleared path to our little bus. And as we drove away, we saw them waving strongly as though to wish us a safe journey.

In the fifties, I found a job tutoring in an institution for neglected and dependent children. I will call it Sleepy Hollow. It was lodged in an old Hudson River estate thirty miles or so north of New York City. The children were black, white, and Puerto Rican. Most had been born into poverty; a few came from middle-class homes that had collapsed as a result of some of the afflictions which can turn ordinary life into a nightmare — loss of jobs, alcoholism, divorce, eruptions into daylight of long-standing incest.

Perhaps half of them had been in trouble with the law, or on the verge of it. A few had spent time in the old Bellevue Hospital in the days when shock treatment was administered nearly as commonly as aspirin. Others had been brought to the institution by a distraught family member who was either too poor to feed one more mouth, or just didn't know what to do with a wild, explosive child. The words *cope* and *handle,* and the mild delusions of grandeur they evoke, had not yet entered popular language and thought.

The children lived in cottages, where they were supposed to be supervised by married couples, mostly in their late fifties, whose main qualifications, with some exceptions, appeared to me to be a combination of stolidity and blandness. They looked as if they'd seen everything and it didn't add up to much.

Quite a few of the children, who ranged in age from eight to seventeen, attended the local elementary and high schools. I was hired to tutor those who were either too fragile or too disruptive to go off the grounds, or who could, but who were falling seriously behind in their school work.

The main house creaked with age and neglect, but from its vast windows, you could stare, if you chose, at the noble Hudson while you waited for your appointment with a worker in the social services department. The air was thickened with the characteristic smell of institutions, a sour and melancholy combination of floor wax and disinfectant. Nearly all the workers had goodwill toward their clients, and a few showed passionate concern. A psychiatrist came once a week for conferences. A minister of no particular denomination held morning services on Sunday in what had been the former owner's private chapel.

Along the banks of the Hudson, above the railroad tracks, among the trees, in spots here and there on the vast, unkempt lawns, the children gathered, living different secret lives. They appeared at meal times, did some of the chores they were supposed to do in their cottage homes, turned up one or two times out of three for their appointments with the social workers, and occasionally drifted into the chapel on Sundays. But theirs was a concealed community within the larger one of Sleepy Hollow. It was said, ruefully, in social services, that the children often did each other more good than their therapists did.

The old-timers threatened the bullies and comforted the wretched in ways that were unequivocal, often physical. They were tough; they didn't waste time or breath on tactful approaches to new members of the community who were terrorists, or else, so miserably afraid, they hid under their beds.

One early evening, as I started up the steps of the old gatekeeper's lodge where my classroom was, I saw nearby a small girl weeping. I learned later that she had been brought to Sleepy Hollow that morning. Three children were gathered around her. A boy was making comical faces at her, stooping, because he was so much taller than she was, to try to make her look at him. Another boy had flung his arm around her narrow shoulders. And the third, an older girl, was holding her fingers, apparently counting them. As I drew closer I heard her say — "This little piggy went to market . . ." The little girl sobbed. The tall boy said, "Cut it out! It don't do no good. You'll use up all your water." The second boy tightened his grip on her and rocked her back and forth. She snuffled. She reached out and touched the intricate cornrows of the girl who held so tightly to the fingers of her other hand. "How do you do that?" she asked between sobs. Suddenly, like a flock of startled birds, they flew off toward a stand of larch trees, holding on to the little girl as though they could physically bear her out of her misery.

Her name was Gloria. That year, she was placed in three foster homes. Each time, she was brought back to Sleepy Hollow. She was eight, skinny and small, but the force of her rage frightened foster parents. She destroyed furniture, china, the clothes she was given, howling at the top of her lungs that she wouldn't. She wouldn't. Her refusal was monumental. She didn't want to leave the other children in the residence. In a black sea of dread, they were a secure island.

One evening, I had supper in her cottage and sat next to her. Everyone except Gloria complained, not unreasonably, about the burnt and acrid-tasting frankfurters. The cottage parents listened placidly and imperturbably. That was their job. Gloria grinned at me and whispered, "I love these hot dogs." I think she would have eaten charcoal as long as she could stay among the children. Her trust in them since three had taken her to the larch trees and delivered her from the terror she felt, brought out her brightness and humor. She was placed, finally, in a foster home where there were many other children. That time, the placement took.

It was the aim of the administration to place as many children as possible. They didn't have much luck with boys or girls over ten.

My classroom in the gatekeeper's lodge was furnished with a splintery table, my desk, small, scarred desks for the children, a blackboard, and a single shelf holding a few battered texts on chemistry and mathematics. I was to tutor them in reading and composition. In most cases, they were far better at arithmetic than I was.

Sometimes I stayed as much as an hour beyond the prescribed time. We would tell stories then. Unlike the concentration camp children, they were eager to talk about their lives. We would also speak of animals, or ghosts or food, anything at all. They liked the high drama of revolting foods: frogs' legs, for example; sea-slugs, which I told them could be found in Chinese markets; or certain highly prized maguey worms in Mexican cuisine. At that time, rattlesnake meat had a brief, I hope, run as a delicacy in this country. Several of the children found a can of it in a grocery in one of the local towns and brought it to me one night, even remembering to bring a can opener. I failed the test gastronomically, but passed it to their satisfaction when I shrieked and pleaded with them to take the can out of my sight.

They liked to hear about my childhood in Cuba. In return, they told me appalling stories of their own early years, of beatings, of being locked in dark places, of setting fires, of tormenting animals and drunks. It was hard to listen. I soon perceived that the neutrality I had assumed was called for was not what they wanted. They needed it, perhaps, from their therapists, but not from me. I reacted pretty much as I felt. It occurred to me that what they would have liked very much was to have heard Charles Dickens read from *Oliver Twist*. It would have confirmed their sense of reality, of the truth of their own lives. It was what they knew, though it was terrible.

There are two boys I remember especially. One was twelve-year-old, illegitimate Danny, who had broken into a neighboring village liquor store one night. He was found by the police, lying among smashed bottles, dead-drunk. He was brought back to Sleepy Hollow where he lay sick and weak for several days. He was a small, thin boy with delicate Irish features. His history was told to me briefly by his social worker. His mother, an alcoholic, had become a prostitute to earn the money to maintain her drinking habit. When Danny was ten, she pushed him out onto the street and locked the door. He hung around for a week, eating out of garbage cans, sleeping in alleys, until the police picked him up. The other children told me he was "bad" to animals.

One evening he was the first to arrive at the gatehouse. He was in a temper, cursing in a way that would seem quaint in these days — a few *damns* and a *hell* or two. When I asked him what was wrong, he told me the minister had reproached him for throwing earthworms into a can of lye.

"I wanted to see what would happen," he explained without a touch of slyness. "You knew what would happen," I retorted. "You don't like what I did, either," he said. "No, I don't," I agreed.

Sensing danger, cats and stray dogs fled at Danny's approach. Someone on the staff had an idea. They got him a small donkey. He tried very hard to knock the donkey senseless. But though he punched it and kicked it, the donkey took to him and followed him faithfully. After a few weeks, he began to love it. I often saw the two of them, the donkey cropping grass, or wandering among bushes to scratch his hide, and Danny, his arm around the animal's bobbing neck, talking to it.

During my year at Sleepy Hollow, Danny, who had seemed only a large, insoluble problem, really began to get better at everything, his schoolwork, his relations with other children, and in his treatment of animals. He was witty. One evening he came to the classroom carrying one of the long bamboo poles the children were allowed to take to the banks of the river and fish. On its hook was an expiring daisy, which he had apparently plucked roots and all, from the ground. Yes, it was for me, he said in his dry little voice, adding that he wouldn't touch a flower with a ten-foot pole.

I was a smoker. He used to try to cadge cigarettes from me. Because the children liked to rummage in my handbag, I kept cigarettes in my pocket. But they had seen me smoking after class on my way to my car.

Danny stayed on one night after the children had gone. "How about giving me a couple of cigarettes?" he asked. "It's almost Christmas." I shook my head. "Just one?" he wheedled. "Not a piece of one," I replied. "Aw — come on!" he begged. "They won't hurt me!"

My heart quickened; it was as if a remote creature had, after a silence that seemed permanent, suddenly spoken its name. What I heard inside his words was his belief that I was concerned about his well-being. I didn't give him a cigarette, but I got permission to take him for a short drive down to the river. The only thing he said was to observe with slight disdain that I didn't have a car radio. When I dropped him off, I saw the donkey emerge from the shadow of some trees and trot along after him as he went toward his cottage.

One night, there was trouble. Two older boys got into a fight in the narrow hall outside the classroom. They had gotten hold of two long barbecue forks. The phone to the main house where there was a night guard was often out of order, and it was that night. In my first moment of panic, I had tried to use it.

I grabbed the boy I knew best by his shirt collar, and holding on to it for dear life, climbed up on one of the tables. I still recall the anguish I felt. I think I said, or rather, cried out, something like, "Is this what thousands of years of human life is to come to? Is this all we are — snarling, murderous things?" This wild, vague oratory and the tears of frustration that were rolling down my cheeks, caught their attention. The fight stopped abruptly. The children stared at me with wonder and considerable amusement. The brother of the boy whose collar I had grabbed came over to me as I sank into a chair, and patted my head. "That's all right," he said soothingly, as though *I* were the child. "Don't worry. It's okay now."

What happened that night remains a mystery to me. Sometimes I've thought the fight stopped because I said *we* instead of *you*. I'll never know.

After I left my job at Sleepy Hollow, I heard that Danny had made friends with an older boy. After lights out, they read *Huckleberry Finn* together with a flashlight. One dark night, they ran away. They made it all the way to Maryland, to the place where the Susquehanna River flows into Chesapeake Bay. They stole a rowboat. They had gotten only a few hundred yards from the shore when the owner of the boat spotted them. They were sent back to Sleepy Hollow. A long time later, when I reread *Huckleberry Finn*, I thought of Danny. I wondered if there was anyone alive who wouldn't have wanted someone to say to him, to her, "Come on up on the raft, Huck, honey. . . ."

Another of my students was Frank, the oldest boy in Sleepy Hollow. He was nearly seventeen, and he attended the local high school. He was tall and thin, quick on his feet and, as he said about himself, made for basketball. But he didn't like sports at all. What he was interested in was outer space.

He had spent most of his life in foster homes. He had a rootless quality; he always seemed at the point of departure. He perched on the edge of his desk and listened tolerantly while I tried to show him what a complete sentence was, but he was thinking of something else.

If someone had told you Frank was a sociopath, which someone had told me, you might have had difficulty attaching that word to Frank. He loved the talking part of those evenings, after the work was done — the stories, the jokes, the drift of spoken memories.

I saw him angry once. That was when the Sleepy Hollow children who went out to schools in the neighborhood were issued special food tickets. It seemed they frequently spent the money they were allotted on candy and cigarettes, instead of lunch. The local kids did, too. Drugs were not available in those days as they are now.

Frank, and the other children, refused to go to their schools until the administration stopped the use of the tickets. It was hard enough for them to be known as institution inmates, but to be so dramatically singled out as they were at that moment when they had to hand over their maroon tickets to the cafeteria cashier was intolerable to them.

They were often bullied and baited by the local children, who exalted themselves and their own circumstances — whatever these might have really been — at the expense of the strangers in their midst, a form of cruelty not restricted to children.

When Frank was seven, he had asked his mother to take him to a movie. She said she couldn't. A friend was driving her to an appointment with a doctor. Frank told her he wished she was dead. She was killed a few hours later in an accident. Frank's father had deserted his family several years earlier. There was no one to take care of Frank and his brother. They began their foster home lives a few weeks after their mother's death.

I don't know how deeply, or in what part of his mind, he felt there to be a fatal connection between his fleeting rage, the wish that had expressed it, and the death that afternoon. I know he suffered — his very abstractedness was a form of suffering.

One night, Frank lingered on the gatehouse porch. He asked me if I had ever worked in another place like Sleepy Hollow. I said no. Then, for some reason, I told him, as I have told you, about the concentration camp children I had met in the high Tatra mountains. I spoke a little about the Holocaust. We sat down on a step. It was a clear night, spring, with a little warmth in the air. The stars were thick.

"I never heard of anything like that," he said. He asked me what would happen to those children in the mountains. I said I didn't know, except what happens to everyone — they would have their lives, they had endured and survived the horror of the camps, and each would make what he or she could of it. He looked up at the sky.

"What's after the stars?" he asked. "What's outside of all that we're looking at?"

I named a few constellations I thought I recognized. Although his grades were low, he'd read an astronomy textbook on his own. He corrected my star guesses twice. "But what do you think about out there?" he urged.

I said there seemed to be a wall in the mind beyond which one couldn't go in imagining infinity — at least, I couldn't. "Me, neither," he said. We sat for a few more minutes, then said goodnight and walked away from the gatehouse, me to my car, and he to the cottage where he would live a few months longer before he ran away and was not heard from again by anyone in Sleepy Hollow.

The children in that residence accepted a certain amount of discipline — do your homework, make your bed, eat the carrots before the cupcake — though they complained noisily about it all. What they hated was to be told what they were. They had a heightened sensitivity to questions that weren't questions at all, but that were rooted in iron-clad assumptions.

There were two or three people on the staff who were pretty sure they knew everything. They had forgotten — if they had ever known — that answers are not always synonymous with truth, which tends to fly just beyond reach in a thousand guises.

Those staff members were imprisoned in their notions as much as the children they met with weekly were imprisoned in case-history terminology. Professions require a system of reference and the language to express it, but the cost to truth is high if there is no reflection on the possibilities beyond that system. "What's outside of all we're looking at?" Frank had asked.

It is a question that appears to be inherent in our species, until we smother it with comfortable certainties. Jonathan Swift wrote that the people of Laputa were fed with "invented, simplified language," and machines were made to "educate . . . pupils by inscribing wafers, causing them to swallow it."

A protocomputer, perhaps — input, output. Can machines tell us what goes on between you and me? As the scientist Dr. Jacob Bronowski once said, a computer cannot be embarrassed or be made to feel regret. It can't feel joy. Lest we turn into machines of certainty, I think we must sustain the suspicion that there's a lot we don't know.

A decade after I left Sleepy Hollow, I was hired by a private preparatory school in New York to teach children who were failing their courses. Most of them were the offspring of alumni and were kept on in the school despite its reputation for placing accomplished students in the most exalted colleges and universities.

The G-group, as my students were called, were separated physically as well as in more subtle social ways from the rest of the student body. Our classroom was in an annex. Except for two or three, most of these children came from homes where they had their own rooms. Their closets were filled with cheerful clothes for every season. They had ice-skates, soccer balls, typewriters — but a list grows tedious. What they had was anything they wanted, or their parents thought they wanted. They were born into families which — whatever their own predilections might have been — valued learning and cultivation. Literature and music and art were as much a part of the environment as regular meals, summer camps in New England, nice clothes, and visits to pediatricians, psychiatrists and dentists when the services of such were called for.

Of course, there were children who didn't give a fig for art, music, and literature. "He won't read anything but baseball scores," a parent would tell me in tones of despair about her seventh-grader, a despair more appropriate to a death in the family than a child's reluctance to wade through *Barnaby Rudge*. These children were burdened not only with material choices; they bore from an early age their parents' fierce ambition that they aim themselves like arrows, not deviating a jot, until they had landed safely in an Ivy League college. This was in the late sixties, so as we know from the student rebellions and all their consequences, that safety was illusory.

Writing about these prep-school students, I recalled the son of an acquaintance who went to Bronx Science, a public high school with an unblemished record of graduating every senior, every year. On graduation day, my acquaintance's son was missing from the parade of seniors accepting their diplomas. He had failed and was obliged to repeat his senior year. But he was in the vicinity, outside on the sidewalk, wearing a T-shirt and jeans, shouting in jubilation and triumph, as the happy families emerged from the ceremony, "I didn't make it! I didn't make it!"

There were obviously profound differences between Gloria, Danny, and Frank, and many of the students in the New York private school. One of the most unpleasant was the privileged children's unquestioning belief that all they had was theirs by right, and that those who had less were somehow inferior. The Sleepy Hollow children hadn't the faintest idea that anything at all was owed them.

Yet, the G-group had something in common with Danny, Gloria, and Frank. They had known failure, too, in their own community. It was a paradox that these G-students were sometimes more interesting as people than their successful contemporaries in the main school. They had a certain gravity, and hardly any of the complacency that makes for endless adolescence.

One of them was a fourteen-year-old boy, Peter. He and his family had fled from Hungary during the uprising in 1956. Each family member took one small possession in their escape. Peter's was a book of Hungarian fairy tales he kept with him wherever he went. I saw it every day on his desk, the pages tattered, the cover faded. He often touched it as though it was a talisman. It was. It had been read to him in his own language, in the days before he had experienced a bitter sense of strangeness and hopelessness.

I began to have the conviction that he couldn't go on with his life unless he could give up the book. He was a lovely boy, courtly, dreamy, gentle. But although he spoke English quite well, he couldn't keep up with any of his studies. He was trying to go backward, to the days when he had been small and happy. Like Frank, he was thinking of something else.

One afternoon, I kept him after class to go over some work. The fairy tale book was there, as always, within his reach, on my desk.

"Why don't you translate one of those stories?" I asked him.

"But I can't," he exclaimed, as though I'd asked him to profane a sacred object. Perhaps I had.

"One of the short ones," I suggested. He looked through

the pages of the book, many of which were clumsily repaired with tape.

"Yes," I said, not knowing quite what I meant.

"But it's better in Hungarian," he said.

"It's always better in the original," I said. "But you could try."

I would like to tell you that he took up my suggestion at once, translated the whole book, made great strides in his school work and escaped the G-group. It didn't happen that way. But he did make an effort with one of the stories, and somehow, that gave him encouragement. He was a brave child. Eventually, he got through the school and went to a small college in the Middle West. The man who was headmaster of the school during the years I taught there once said to me, "It is not unreasonable to limp in this world."

I ask these questions: What do pessimism or optimism have to do with Richard, who lived his childhood, day after day for six years, in a concentration camp? With Gloria, Danny, and Frank? With Peter? With these living presences, immanent with human soul?

Are their lives, and ours, like sad? Like baffling? Like rapturous?

The ebbing away of religious belief has resulted in the loss of the language we need to express deep and serious feelings about our lives. How are we to give voice to despair, to exaltation and redemption?

But we can turn to great poets, great writers, to help us speak of life, of its mysteries. They, too, have reverence for the gods, and implicit in their work is the belief, as it is in religion, that everything that happens is extraordinarily important.

And so I would like to end this talk with the words of a great writer, Franz Kafka, who wrote:

"You can hold back from the suffering of the world, you have free permission to do so, and it is in accordance with your nature, but perhaps this very holding back is the one suffering you could have avoided."

Introduction to David Macaulay

DAVID MACAULAY HAS BEEN acknowledged by both critics and architectural historians as one of the great contemporary chroniclers of construction. His series starting with *Cathedral* and proceeding through *City, Pyramid, Underground,* and *Castle,* was published, one per year from 1973 through 1977, to resounding reviews and awards. Each of those books takes the reader — by vivid drawings and concise, clear texts — through the planning, building, and motivation behind monuments representing entire civilizations. Macaulay's holistic approach includes tools, materials, engineering techniques, social hierarchies, rituals, and life-styles that generated, and were in turn affected by, structures requiring up to a century of coordinated effort. The visual perspectives he uses — aerial, cross-section, or interior — permit prime views of a culture as well as a building. Furthermore, amid the grandiosities of crenelated towers and geared arches, Macaulay is not afraid to tackle the real historical question burning in every child's mind — and adult's, if truth were known: Where did they all go to the bathroom?

After winning several Caldecott Honors, a Boston

Globe–Horn Book citation, a Christopher Award, an American Institute of Architects medal, a Deutscher Jugendliteraturpreis, and a Dutch Silver Slate Pencil Award for these five landmark titles, David demonstrated his versatility with two spoofs on his own and others' reverence for monumental undertakings. *Great Moments in Architecture* and *Motel of the Mysteries* celebrate the ridiculous with parodies on architecture, archeology, research, and museums. One of his funniest books, *Unbuilding,* recounts the dismantling of the Empire State Building by an oil prince for use in the Arabian desert. The neat technological explanations combined with the entertaining satire manage to convey an enormous amount about skyscrapers — both constructing and wrecking them — and the illustration features some of Macaulay's most breathtaking scenes.

This blend of the informative and the entertaining has become a Macaulay trademark. His books evidence the fact that science is an art, requiring the power of the imagination, the leap of intuitive, as well as of technical, understanding. The best work involves play. We need inventive space to balance hard-worked knowledge. David's book *The Way Things Work* is a volume of mammoth imagination, energy, and humor. It undertakes the modest assignment of explaining everything mechanical, and it succeeds, with mirth. It justifies every critic's belief that good nonfiction is storytelling at its best. *The New York Times* reviewed it favorably for adults in its daily paper, and for children in its Sunday *Book Review.* Another unusual characteristic of Macaulay's work is its accessibility to a broad age range, from elementary school, college, and graduate students to adults browsing in bookstores. He proves the maxim that the greatest books speak effectively at different levels of understanding.

Volumes 3 and 14 of *Children's Literature Review* quote twenty-one oversize pages of critics' relentless praise for Macaulay's work, and the *Review* is selective. Nellvena Duncan Eutsler has a long and thoughtful analysis of his works in *The Dictionary of Literary Biography,* which she concludes with the following summary: "Macaulay's first books may be concerned simply with the process of building and construction, but in his later books he strives to develop meaning and theme. He is interested in more than construction; he is also interested in preservation and education."[1] I suppose this is high praise, but what I find most commendable about David Macaulay is that he's interested in *Why the Chicken Crossed the Road.*

He may even tell you that now. David Macaulay.

David Macaulay

The Truth About Nonfiction
May 5, 1989

PART ONE: The first portion of this evening's talk is composed entirely of facts. It is May 5th, 1989. This is Chicago. I am here and you are here listening to me. But I have an excuse. Long ago I received a letter from Liz Huntoon inviting me to give the 1989 Zena Sutherland Lecture. I was immediately overwhelmed by two more facts. The first, there isn't a lecture anywhere in the world in anyone else's name that I would rather give, although I would be willing, contrary to unpopular opinion, to consider perhaps a little talk at one of those — what are they called? — Caldecott things.

And the second is that included in the letter was the list of distinguished individuals who have preceded me as ZSLs — Zena Sutherland Lecturers. I was flattered into reckless submission (which is how I get most of my more interesting assignments) and hastily scrawled and returned an illegible and probably illiterate response. I hoped they wouldn't change their minds once they had deciphered it, though chances of either seemed pretty slim. Since the actual event was eight months away, I simply entertained in the deep recesses of my mind the fiction of my presentation. It would be intellectually demanding, yet rewarding. It would sparkle with wit and be laced with candor. It would be, in short, unforgettable but legal.

I had no idea what I was actually going to say, but felt no pressure at that time to trouble myself with trifles. Which brings up another fact: All good things must come to an end, eventually.

Immediately after receiving the invitation and before I could say *The Way Things Work,* and shortly before anybody else could find a copy, I was off on what seemed like an almost endless series of promotional engagements for that recently survived endeavor. I traveled from Edinburgh to Seattle selling my wares and telling anyone who would listen why it is important to know how the lawn sprinkler and the can opener work and how simple the computer *really* is.

I spoke of mechanics and molecules and Mammoths. I responded to the same questions and comments over and over again with saintly patience and unswerving enthusiasm.

"Mr. Macaulay, I expected a much older man," to which I would say either, "I'm getting there as fast as I can," or "I used to be older, but things have been going well." It gets them every time. We both laugh. Ha ha ha. Next question. "I've been having trouble with my toilet. Do you have any idea what the problem might be?" I suggest they are probably using it incorrectly and refer them to *Motel of the Mysteries* for detailed instructions. The best thing about interviews is that you're safely back on the plane before they start thinking about what you've said.

In early November, the tour took me from Washington

to Chicago, where Zena and I had a chance to discuss this very event. I wanted to try out some of my ideas for what I might actually say on May fifth. Given the standards of erudition which had already been set, I offered to present my exhaustive study of humor in the works of Ibsen. A tad too intellectual, her glance implied. How about Shaving in Space: Which way do whiskers point in a weightless environment, or what do whiskers weigh in a pointless environment? Too technical, said she. I tried again, only this time, I dropped the big one — the one I'd been holding back. Children in Sports: 1847 to 1903, at which point Zena thoughtfully though firmly suggested that I simply discuss what I am supposed to know something about: nonfiction. It was, as they say, as if a great weight had been lifted from my shoulders. But little did I know how little I knew. The irony is that for sixteen years I had been merrily contributing to NF shelves and yet, I had never actually bothered to identify NF. From that moment on, I resolved to be on the lookout for clues. My mind immediately shot back to the night before.

The trip from Washington to Chicago had taken ten hours, thanks to some nonfictional meteorological activity along the route. When, at one o'clock in the morning, I discovered my room at the Ambassador East was no longer available, an assertion which the next day I discovered was fiction, I was directed to a small nonfiction hotel on Wabash, where one can still stay in the heart of the Windy City for only forty-five — count them, forty-five — dollars per night. Everyone I passed on my way to my room was pure nonfiction. The lamp shade through which the bulb had at some point melted itself was nonfiction. The last two rings that held up the shower curtain were nonfiction. Eureka! I realized, as I thought back on that unforgettable night, that I had inadvertently struck the mother lode. The very heart of nonfiction. What a break. Even the dreams I had that short night were 100 percent nonfiction. And this was really just the beginning of my tour. What else awaited this unwitting victim of NF?

As I continued my travels, I became aware of the number of hotel elevators with no button number thirteen, and yet when I counted from the street, there always appeared to be a thirteenth floor. I learned that not calling a floor the thirteenth, even though it is in the very place where a thirteenth floor would normally be found, is to eliminate the thirteenth floor. The power of words. NF.

In my Denver hotel, arrival at each floor was announced in the elevator by a beep which I found strangely familiar. It was exactly the same kind of tone that our microwave oven makes when the food is ready to be removed, or at least turned over. Every time the door opened between my floor, the eleventh, and the lobby, I wondered what would reach in. I could feel my temperature rising, my collar tightening. I even found myself slowly revolving when there was no one else in the elevator. I remembered those stories of poodles in the microwave that somehow exploded before their curly little pompoms were dry. Mind over matter, I told myself. Call it fiction if all else fails.

By December 10, the tour was finished and they let me come home for Christmas — a holiday interrupted by only two trips to New York to do *Good Morning America* and *CBS This Morning.* You never saw me on *Good Morning America,* although my mother and a number of her former friends watched every one of those shows for a week and a half in hopes of seeing the segment. It was dropped in favor of other things, including a visit with a duck from the Columbus Zoo with whom I actually shared a few pleasant moments in the green room eating crackers. I was particularly struck by the duck's stupidity. After all, here it was, less than a week before Christmas dinner, and this flighty critter was munching down the makings of stuffing as fast as it could. Sometime in January, when they finally decided to air that insightful and truly arresting gem of technological repartee, they realized that the host and I were surrounded by poinsettias, which is great for Christmas week viewing but seems strangely nostalgic if not downright tacky by New Year's Day. When they beckoned me back to do it all over, I firmly declined, at which point Houghton Mifflin's adult promotion director is reported to have leapt from the fifth floor of the Park Street offices, all of which is why you never saw me on *Good Morning America* and probably never will.

So now I had a few examples of personally experienced NF in hand, but I had promised to reveal the truth about nonfiction. A no-holds-barred, gloves-off, comprehensive, let-it-all-hang-out exposé. I needed more information, I needed a definition. I went confidently to the dictionary, which informed me that "nonfiction is prose works other than fiction." Not one to be brushed off so easily, I recalled Basil Rathbone's uncanny instinct for penetrating the seemingly obvious and backed up to fiction.

"Fiction is a literary work whose content is produced by the imagination and is not necessarily based on fact." I thought I had it. Through an ingenious process of extrapolation, I decided to define nonfiction as follows: a literary work (I like the sound of that) whose content was based primarily on fact and communicated with imagination.

Like any good scientist, I tested my definition whenever I had the chance. But it was a headline on one of those tabloids you can't help perusing while waiting in the check-out line with your milk and charcoal briquettes that clinched it for me. It read: DONOR WANTS KIDNEY BACK! Perfect, nay, inspiring, nonfiction. But the euphoria slowly began to fade. I was becoming increasingly uneasy about one word in my definition, a word I have already introduced this evening. Some of you may know it as the "F" word — FACT. What is a fact? How could I present my definition of nonfiction to you without feeling that every word in it was reliable?

Back to the dictionary: "A fact is something known with certainty. Something asserted as certain." (Assert: "To state or express positively; affirm.") But assertion and therefore facts do not, it seems, nonfiction make. Neville Chamberlain asserted. Oliver North asserted. Ronald Reagan with a teleprompter asserted and then forgot. If a fact is in fact so unreliable, upon what kind of foundation does nonfiction stand? You can't fool around when it comes to foundations! I know that from bedrock up.

I read on. Fact: "Something that has been objectively verified." (Objective: "Of or having to do with a material object as distinguished from a mental concept, idea or belief, having actual existence or reality, uninfluenced by emotion, surmise, or personal prejudice, based on observable phenomena.") Observable phenomena! Doesn't that have to do with seeing? I know from having taught drawing and illustration for the past fifteen years that a lot of people don't know how to look, and therefore, often don't see. And even when an entire class looks at the same thing, they often see surprisingly different things! That would imply that the same fact could be seen differently. In that case, is it still a fact? Or are only certain people qualified to observe the observable phenomena?

It was at this point that I first began to seriously entertain the notion of not defining nonfiction. I could simply call it the opposite of fiction which, as you will recall, is not necessarily based on fact. Then I would be free to present nonfiction by giving a talk on fiction, only reading it backward.

Fearing some confusion with this approach, I decided instead to begin my presentation by giving examples of nonfiction instead of defining it, thereby letting you decide what it is — where it starts and where it stops.

Vinyl siding is nonfiction. Porta-Johns are nonfiction. Cinder blocks are nonfiction. All this can be verified through a little basic research. You might be interested to know how cinder blocks or CBs evolved into their present twin cavity, dull gray, pebbled texture. Who invented them? And why? While many specific details remain lost, the earliest existence of cinder blocks was supposedly recorded at a neighborhood square dance in the Middle West. No artifacts were ever unearthed, and it is now widely believed that these were not actually CBs as we know them today, but rather overcooked Rice Krispie squares. Perhaps because cinder blocks are nonfiction, they are usually buried behind either a skin of bricks (also nonfiction) or a plastic stuccolike surface over a wallboard product called Dryvit which is very much fiction no matter how you install it. Regardless of which material is used to cover the cinder blocks, the result is always fiction. A formula emerged which I share with you now. Two nonfictions equal a fiction. A fiction and a nonfiction equal a fiction. Those of you mathematically inclined have undoubtedly deduced, then, that two fictions must equal a nonfiction. For proof, I suggest we just look at the last national election. If more proof is required that two fictions equal a nonfiction — look at the results: candidate George Bush and candidate Dan Quayle *are* the administration!

It may be impossible to satisfactorily define nonfiction without the help of comparison. Here is a potentially useful rule of thumb which I learned long ago. On your basic hard-cover book is a dust jacket. The condition of that protective promotional piece, or PPP, depends to a great extent on the popularity of the book, the care of the bookseller, and the whim of the post office. While definitely nonfiction, condition is irrelevant to this particular rule of thumb. Front-flap copy, which, almost without exception, is located on the front flap of every PPP, is basically a profusion of hyperbole related as loosely as necessary to the content of the book and is invariably pure fiction regardless of the persuasion of the text it promotes. Back-flap copy, usually found at the other end of the PPP, which contains embarrassingly irrelevant biographical detail, is painfully nonfiction. Remember — fiction up front, nonfiction behind. Let flap copy be your guide.

Thankfully, all of this hemming and hawing may soon be unnecessary, thanks to some startling advancements in technology. During one of the many tedious flights I found myself on during the grand tour, I willingly accepted from the flight attendant's pile of magazines an apparently unopened copy of *Library Frontier — The Journal of the Bibliofuturist*. I was intrigued by the possibility of oxymoronic enlightenment. I refer now to one article in particular. It described a new generation of satellites being developed jointly by NASA and the Library of Congress to fly over libraries and schools, distinguishing fiction from nonfiction and tallying the results. It was to be part of a system called Strategic Decimal Inspection, or SDI. The article went on to say that these same satellites could easily be programmed to actually identify good fiction and nonfiction from bad fiction and nonfiction. *Bad,* it described as impenetrable, incomprehensible, incompetent or boring — in other words, prose untainted by imagination.

I was immediately sympathetic to the cause. Each satellite was to be equipped with highly sensitive antennae which would pick up snoring in the vicinity of a book during a generally accepted nonsleeping time. Sensing the signal, the satellite would activate and aim a laser beam, which in turn would promptly vaporize the offending publication. As a precaution, special protective deflectors could be placed over good books by honest readers who appreciate the finer things but fear they might not be able to stay awake. The only real danger mentioned in the article was that posed by vigilante programmers. Although thought to be relatively few in number, these zealous and morally superior individuals could reprogram SDI to pass over schools and libraries distinguishing approved books from unapproved books, laser-editing the offensive passages, books, and even hapless librarians. Unfortunately, there was no suggestion in the article that some comparable system could be put into effect over textbook and trade publishing houses, which might eliminate many of the worst offenders before they ever saw the light of day.

So, where does all this leave us in our factual investigation of nonfiction? Fiction is the opposite of nonfiction. Nonfiction is based on facts. Facts are anybody's guess. Be not dismayed, however. There is one very simple avenue we have not yet traveled. In England, the kind of books I make are not referred to as either fiction or nonfiction, but rather as information books. I looked up *information* and discovered it is the communication of knowledge. With my fingers crossed, I then looked up *knowledge*. The word *fact* was nowhere to be seen.

This concludes the academic portion of this evening's presentation.

∾

Part Two. A visual interlude: engaging the reader/viewer any way you can:

1. *Cathedral* slides: giving sequence and illustrating structure while responding to the drama inherent in architecture; perspective.

2. *Underground* slides: information (manholes, sewers, etc.) not known for its immediate appeal; reading surface clues and visualizing the invisible; variety of points of view and dramatic perspective.

3. *Unbuilding* slides: helicopter crane lift — putting the reader in the picture as active participant rather than passive viewer.

4. *Amazing Brain* slides: following information from the eye to the brain required tremendous simplification — making images as bold and clear as possible; magnification without little people; humor that enlivens the reading experience without compromising the integrity or accuracy of the material; a recognizable although unlikely subject —

> Light upside down to retina
> to optic nerve
> to optic chiasm

to lateral geniculate body parts of thalamus
through fibers of the optic radiation
to visual cortex
into layer 4 of visual cortex (b and w indicates left/
     right dominance)
into orientation slabs so that angles and therefore
     shapes can be recorded and recognized
into single cell sends out nerve impulse
through insulated axon (some over three feet long)
to dendrites of other cells
at synaptic connections transfer of chemicals from
     synaptic button upsets electrical balance on
     receptor cell, sends the message along
spreads through cortex;
David recognizes his mother.

5. *Amazing Garden* slides: fueling up.

6. *The Way Things Work* slides: developing methods of presentation, through learning the information and understanding relationships; selection of broad concepts, rather than specific function, to link machines by the way they work rather than what they do; looking again at the familiar.

7. *BAAA* slides: I didn't know how strong my subconscious feelings are about television until I pulled these slides together and realized how many times TVs appear in this book that Judith Viorst would not give to a child she loves.[2]

Welcome to PART THREE of this evening's program, entitled "The Truth About My Information Books." Perhaps the most important reason for spreading information is to create a basis from which we can confidently question information. Learning how to learn may be a more familiar way of putting it. People communicate whatever they wish us to know in very specific ways and for very specific reasons. I — through my books and even, dare I say it, through my little talks — am no exception. Not to question both the methods of and motives for dissemination of particular information is not to get the whole story. Let's look at newspapers and magazines for a moment. Forget headlines and advertisements; we know that there is nothing accidental about them. The fact is that nothing in print or, for that matter, in any other form of communication, is accidental. Everything produced by people is biased. It's unavoidable, natural, and desirable. Whether it's the way a story is told, the mood created, what is emphasized and what isn't, the question we must always ask ourselves is what was the writer's or photographer's or illustrator's point of view? Where were they standing both literally and metaphorically? What were they trying to say and *why*?

By remaining visually and intellectually alert — in other words, seeing — at least we will know when, how, and why we're being manipulated so that we can enjoy it when appropriate and reject it when necessary.

So why do I create information books in the first place? Much of the answer, not surprisingly, lies in my own childhood. I grew up in a house in which things were always being made. It was a small row house in the north of England. We didn't have a workroom in the basement. We didn't have a basement, for that matter. But I knew a man who had a basement. It was damp and very dark down there. In it he kept a working model of a steam traction engine which I only once saw in action but never forgot. In my house, when something needed to be made, either the table was cleared or, if it was something big, furniture was moved. My father worked mostly with wood, new wood — he still doesn't like having to mess around with old wood — and a few hand tools. I don't remember a single electric tool. Once for Christmas he made me a toy train; another time he made some easels for my school.

Somewhere along the line, I acquired my own hand tools, which he taught me to use and care for. My mother knitted and sewed to keep us clothed, and she baked and entered contests occasionally, making us eat the confections that didn't quite make it, one of which I remember to this day whenever I'm offered a piece of cake I can't readily identify. We were guinea pigs. But she also taught us how to make things like embroidery — I did a bee once — and tea. I would come home from school for lunch and if there was enough time before heading back, she would draw pictures from our favorite stories. I'll never forget her Cinderella running down the stairs semi-slipperless. I'm sure she drew every single step. It was astounding. No wonder I drew at school.

Another direct result of having a fairly small house, although I never thought of it as small at the time, was that I played outside a lot. At the end of the street was a wooded area with a stream. Across the stream was a cemetery where we built forts with dried-out wreaths. I watched frog spawn grow into frogs and hid in the root systems of the larger trees. I went to school through those woods every day looking for unusual rocks, setting paper on fire with my magnifying glass, and finding on very special occasions bits of animal skeletons, moles and mice mostly. It's hardly surprising that I still consider *The Wind in the Willows* nonfiction.

When it rained and I had to entertain myself indoors, I

was let loose in the sitting room — which was normally only used when there was company and otherwise just passed through on the way to the stair. There I made ski lifts out of leftover bobbins and thread, which traveled up to the curtain rods taking plastic soldiers with them. Or I constructed cranes with my Meccano set or made paper models of things to do with the railroad. Whatever I made, it all had one thing in common: It all in some way worked. When I pulled or cranked one thing, something somewhere else moved, and the entire process could be watched.

I never owned a book that wasn't in some way an information book. In fact, I don't think there is such a thing as a noninformation book, with the possible exception of certain IRS publications, but my most important official information book was given to me in 1956. That year, I collected money for Methodist missionaries every Saturday morning for several months, and for pulling in the grand total of about ten dollars (please remember my subscribers only pledged about two to five cents a week), *The Encyclopaedia of Science for Boys and Girls* was my reward. It had everything from simple machines, to echoes, to types of trees and cloud formations. It even had a picture and paragraph in the back about something called space travel. It changed my life. On one page called *biggest, fastest, tallest*, etc., was a picture of the Empire State Building. It looked gigantic. It looked fabulous. Only much later did I realize that one reason why it looked so big was that it was drawn at a different scale to the buildings clustered around its base, and it also never actually touched the ground. It sort of faded out. Not only was it huge in my ten-year-old eyes, it was magical. The power of illustration!

All of these incidents and influences were part of an ideal childhood. I learned about process — that things are made or grow in specific ways for specific reasons — and I came to feel that knowing about the process made appreciation of the subject that much greater. My curiosity to know why things look or behave the way they do can be traced directly to the first ten years.

Enough of this nostalgia, already. Why else do I make information books? Two answers here. First, it still gives me indescribable pleasure to learn things I didn't know, and I'm not expecting to run out of possibilities. Second answer: I believe it is genuinely useful to share this enthusiasm with as many people as possible, either to rekindle a curiosity they may have had or to encourage one that is growing, or even perhaps to plant one where it might otherwise never exist. That sounds a bit presumptuous, I know, but what the heck. I'm a regular Johnny Appleseed with Newtonian aspirations.

When it comes time to choose a subject, I will only select something I can be reasonably sure of enjoying for as long as it takes to create the book. While it might be a good idea, for one reason or another, to do this book or that book, if I don't care enough about the subject, my contribution to my readers will invariably fall short. And who's got time to waste either creating something which you know isn't getting your best, or reading something which you know wasn't given the best? Judging by what's available, the answer is lots of people. But I try increasingly hard not to be one of them. My books are designed to impart information. Sometimes, I simplify complicated pieces of architecture and systems to demystify and make accessible but never to reduce or denigrate. Sometimes, I encourage and even coerce my readers into looking again at the familiar and, I hope, appreciating it. Whichever way I go, the purpose remains the same — to emphasize the common sense and logic behind the creation of most made things, in order to remind and reassure my readers of their own imaginative and practical potential.

If I contribute to this thing called Knowledge, it is because I encourage and insist that our brains and eyes remain continually in touch with each other. I teach drawing and illustration for exactly the same reason — not so much to make people better draftsmen, but to make them better communicators, to help them see better in order to help others see better. You've got it. It's a conspiracy. As long as people remain curious, I'm not worried. But not looking with our eyes and questioning with our minds ultimately discourages curiosity. And a lack of curiosity leads in turn to not seeing.

On one level, the results of not seeing are ugly buildings, endless rows of neon signs, advertising agencies (although they exist to help us see in a very specific and self-serving way), political marketing consultants, Smurfs, Barbie dolls, and, in general, mediocrity. But on another much deeper level, it threatens to turn us into pod people, insensitive, incapable, and ultimately helpless victims in a world of increasing complexity and decreasing humanity.

The problem of not really seeing sounds inoffensive enough at first. But as soon as not paying attention becomes a habit, we start accepting the built environment without question. As technology becomes more sophisticated, we are less and less able to actually see how things work. Switches and buttons are hidden behind shiny metal plates. Just flip or push, but please, don't ask questions. The skeletons of steel and concrete that support our buildings are eventually sheathed in envelopes of glass and deli-slices of granite and travertine. *I* think most new buildings look far more interesting under construction than they do complete! The process in most cases is much more appealing than the finished product. It is very important that we are able to visualize the structure, once it has been covered, so that we don't mistake the skin for the building — surface for substance. If we aren't aware of it, we won't ask about it. And "don't ask" eventually becomes "don't even be curious." Visual complacency rears its ugly head, and each time it does, we humans lose a little ground.

A major contributor to our visual desensitizing is that much-maligned, immensely powerful, and incredibly underutilized glowing box around which so much of daily life seems to revolve. First of all, just look at the programming we put up with. We try to compensate by purchasing programs from the British, who in turn feed their audiences *The Dukes of Hazzard* and *The Monkees.* You see how international the problem of visual illiteracy has become. And here, we get back to that blurring of fiction and nonfiction.

Look at the evening news for a moment. On one network, it opens and closes with movie music. It's not surprising when you recall it was composed by a man who has built his reputation writing movie music. Don't misunderstand me here. I'm all for the movie music — at the movies! And speaking of movies, we know all too well that stories presented on the news by news personalities, with nifty graphics and live footage, often end up as the basis of made-for-TV films. And we are now accustomed to seeing incidents invented for TV being imitated in real life and ending up as news stories, presumably to be made into films for TV to be imitated and so on and so on. Consider the hand-held camera for a moment. As journalism, that shaky unpolished image, filmed under pressure and perhaps even at risk of life, has taken us into the midst of countless tragedies and disasters. We associate the look of the footage with urgency and danger and truth. In filmmaking, this look is a very effective device for reducing the distance between audience and action and more important, between fact and fiction. It gets harder and harder — and possibly even pointless — to distinguish between news and entertainment.

Because of this blurring of boundaries, along with the neutralizing of innate curiosity accomplished by either carelessly or intentionally covering up the workings of our world, it has become increasingly important to practice the art of seeing.

Like many of you here tonight, I grew up at a time when more of the things that surround us every day and on which we are often completely dependent could be somewhat understood just by watching them. It was also a time in which you could *take the time* to watch. This is no longer so easy, and therefore, the importance of working at visual connection is, I think, that much greater.

Whether I chronicle the hundred-year-long process of building a Gothic cathedral or try to present the millionth-of-a-second machinations of a microchip, I am attempting to involve and engage my readers in the unavoidable — and I think mostly understandable — complexities of the world around us. How easy it would be, though, given the speed at which things change in this seemingly out-of-control world, just to say — "Oh, the hell with it. It's all too confusing. I don't have time to think about it, and besides, it's all much too complicated anyway."

As soon as we stop asking questions, we lose both the ability and the right to control our own destiny. Without curiosity, there is no hope. That's why I do what I do, and I will continue to do it until I run out of time, and that's a fact.

NOTES

1. Nellvena Duncan Eutsler, *American Writers for Children Since 1960: Poets, Illustrators, and Nonfiction Authors,* vol. 61 of *The Dictionary of Literary Biography,* ed. Glenn E. Estes (Detroit: Gale Research, 1987), p. 188.
2. Judith Viorst, Review of *BAAA, New York Times Book Review,* December 1, 1985.

Introduction to Jean Fritz

JEAN FRITZ HAS MADE history in more ways than one. More than any other writer, she has made history-writing for children a process of researching primary sources. Hers has not been the conventional route of synthesizing and regurgitating well-known facts and figures for children's edification — and infinite boredom. Her own enthusiasm for combing records, diaries, letters, and other sources for odd tidbits of information about long-ago incidents and personalities injects her books with a tone of discovery.

More than any other writer, she has brought to history-writing for children a sense of story that does not distract from the essentially captivating facts. Her perception, selection, and development of true stories has given shape to biography that ranges from a lighthearted look at the quirks of America's founding fathers to serious studies of those whom U.S. history caught in its cruelest dilemmas.

More than any other writer, she has imbued history-writing for children with an honesty that replaces the kind of superficial adulation that equates leadership with didactic role models. She acknowledges to children that even the greatest human beings are still only human, a condition that enhances their achievements with struggles common to us all.

And finally, more than any other writer, she has injected history-writing for children with a sense of humor, not in a cutesy effort to sweeten reality, but as an inherent part of reality. She sees that, on balance, human beings are a funny lot despite their tragic blunders, and she delivers the evidence with wit and style. Her humorous perspective provides a sense of balance sadly missing from many accounts of the past, and it makes the specifics unforgettable. She opens her book *And Then What Happened, Paul Revere?* with the kind of details for which children comb through *Ripley's Believe It or Not:*

> In 1735 there were in Boston 42 streets, 36 lanes, 22 alleys, 1,000 brick houses, 2,000 wooden houses, 12 churches, 4 schools, 418 horses (at last count), and so many dogs that a law was passed prohibiting people from having dogs that were more than 10 inches high. But it was difficult to keep dogs from growing more than 10 inches, and few people cared to part with their 11- and 12-inch dogs, so they paid little attention to the law. In any case there were too many dogs to count.[1]

Fritz continues her account to reveal that the false teeth that Paul Revere whittled out of hippopotamus tusk were as effective as his silversmithing; that he doodled in his Day Book; that (according to a granddaughter's testimony) he forgot to bring cloth to muffle the oars for his secret row across the Charles River *and* forgot his spurs for the big ride to warn the citizenry of approaching Brit-

ish troops; that after the war he made 398 church bells
and had trouble collecting payment for them; that five of
Revere's babies died, as so many babies did in those days.
Fritz draws her picture of Revere, the way she does of Ben
Franklin, John Hancock, Samuel Adams, Patrick Henry,
and even King George, with rhythmic language and a sus-
penseful pace crafted to hold readers or listeners in thrall.
Her work on Pocahontas, Benedict Arnold, Sam Houston,
and others extends that skill to a fuller exploration of
complex history-makers as individuals.

Beyond her contributions to history-writing itself, she
has made history by living it with an awareness keen
enough to translate her own unusual life story into historical fiction. Her childhood in China during the turbulent
years of 1915 to 1928 gave her an outsiders' view both of
her own culture and of another, an understanding of social
conflicts that is at once broadly international and deeply
personal. Even stories that seem remote from her own
experience have benefited from the intensity of that awareness. One of her earliest books, *The Cabin Faced West*,
focuses acutely on a pioneer child's sense of isolation, the
same sense of isolation so vividly reflected in Fritz's autobiographical novel set in China and entitled *Homesick*.
After the protagonist of *Homesick* learns of her baby sister's death and watches two coolies carry the small coffin
down a mountain path for burial in Hankow, she cries to
her father, "You and mother will never understand. I was
waiting for Miriam to grow. I knew she'd understand. She
was the only one. I was counting on her. I *needed* her." (p.
76) That was the loneliness of missionary children matur-
ing in a distant culture-outside-a-culture. In this and many
other scenes, Fritz has given children a voice in history, as
well as giving history a voice for children.

Jean Fritz has been writing books since 1954, and she has a history of getting awards for them: Among many other citations for her works, twenty-three of which are now in print, *Homesick* was a Newbery Honor Book and a Boston Globe–Horn Book Honor Book as well as receiving an American Book Award and Christopher Award in 1983; *The Double Life of Pocahontas* won the Boston Globe–Horn Book Award in 1984; and for the body of her work, Jean Fritz was awarded the Regina Medal in 1985 and the Laura Ingalls Wilder Medal in 1986, along with being nominated for the Hans Christian Andersen Medal. These awards, however, are just names and dates without the real voice that you are about to hear now. Jean Fritz.

Jean Fritz

The Known and the Unknown: An Exploration into Nonfiction
May 4, 1990

I HAVE OFTEN WISHED that there were another word for nonfiction. Although Webster defines nonfiction as a branch of literature, a non-anything hardly sounds strong enough to pass muster as a branch. What then? Is nonfiction simply the opposite of fiction, a kind of catch-all for leftovers on the literature tree? Yet fiction and nonfiction, in spite of the wall that separates them, both draw from a common ancestry. Good nonfiction is invariably related to *story* and, like fiction, it travels from the known to the unknown, from the unknown to the known, for all stories, whether fiction or nonfiction, are set in time. And where there is time, there is mystery; where there is time, there is surprise. And here, I think, is where the world of education goes wrong. Whenever it glides over the surprises, whenever it ignores the suspense, whenever it insists on presenting pat answers instead of probing into questions, it is weakening the power of nonfiction on which much of education is based.

As human beings, we thrive on astonishment. Whatever is unknown quickens us, delivers us from ourselves, impels us to investigate, inspires us to imagine, drives us sometimes to extravaganza, sometimes to outright fraud. I like to step back to the time of Columbus and try to experience a world in which the known geography was perched on the edge of vast regions marked on maps, "Here Be Dragons." What would it be like to believe there were dragons thrashing about on your horizon? Of course, in such a time someone was bound to fake a personal knowledge of that big Unknown. And so it was that a French physician who called himself Sir John Mandeville came out with a travel book describing people with umbrella feet, people with eyes on their shoulders. Columbus, eager to believe, believed and took Mandeville's book with him when he went exploring. Indeed, he would have felt far less threatened by the extravagant creatures which he had come to expect than by a New World which he did not expect and refused to recognize. When you are making forays into the Unknown, it is wise to expect the unexpected, because invariably that is what you get.

I often think of my distant ancestor, one Abraham Teagarden, who lived in Prussia in a town which specialized in sword making. Abraham was a whetter; his job was to sharpen sword blades. He expected to go right on whetting in his little Prussian town, until one day, he saw a pamphlet written by Benjamin Franklin, who was campaigning to bring people to Pennsylvania. It was warm in Pennsylvania, like Naples, Franklin said; there was plenty of land, plenty of work for craftsmen, plenty of opportunity. Abraham picked up his whetting tools and before long, there he was in Pennsylvania, all ready to make swords. If he was disappointed that Pennsylvania did not offer a big market for swords and was not as warm on a winter's day as he had imagined, he left no record of it. We see him

next, poling a ferry back and forth across the Mononga-
hela River, fighting Indians, registering a claim for a piece
of land. All unexpected, but I like to think that Abraham
had the heart for the Unknown.

What about young people today? They have seen our
planet become crowded and polluted; they have watched
men walk on the moon, but I worry sometimes that they
have lost contact with the Unknown. Has their sense of
wonder been blunted? Are they susceptible only to the
astonishment offered by television hype? Are they uncomfortable with the Unknown, so that they reach into the
occult for answers?

This last fall, I spent three unforgettable weeks in a
landscape about as far removed from what I consider the
Known World as I could reasonably get. I was speaking to
remote Eskimo schools huddled beside the Bering Sea, in
sight of Siberia, just under the Arctic Circle. There I was,
in a tiny Cessna plane flying into what seemed to be the
final resting place of infinity — silent, stark, and breathtaking. This was old land-bridge country and, looking
down from the air, I felt what a small bit of time had
actually lapsed since men were walking across this northern edge of the Bering Sea. It is easy to restore that land
bridge in one's mind. Islands are still visible under only a
few feet of water; water wells up in the tundra as if the
question of supremacy had not finally been resolved.
Moreover, memory of those early men and women lies
buried just below the surface of the ground, sometimes
only knee deep. Around every village there are holes where
natives dig and find souvenirs of their ancestors, artifacts
made of whalebone and ivory which they sell to visitors
from the outside.

And what, I asked myself, would it feel like to be a child and live in this infinity? The first thing I found out was that you would be sleepy. When you came to school, you would struggle to be on time and you might not make it. At every chance, you would put your head down on your desk and close your eyes. You live in a crowded shacklike house with a TV set and you watch TV long, long into the night. Every night. Indeed, in such small quarters where the adults are watching, you can hardly avoid it. A teacher in one school had taught her fifth- and sixth-graders the meaning of the word *utopia* and asked them to write their own ideas of utopia. The papers were hung in the hall. The most direct response was by John. "John's Utopia," he wrote. "I want to marry early and sleep late." Many utopias were similar to John's; few reached much farther afield.

I thought of what Annie Dillard once wrote: "We still and always want waking. We should amass half dressed in long lines like tribesmen and shake gourds at each other, to wake up; instead we watch television and miss the show."

But we all know people, children and adults alike, who live in the most populated areas all over our country, trapped in worlds equally restricted, people who are missing the show.

In the few weeks I was in Alaska, I had, of course, a very limited view. I didn't see any of the villages on the occasion of a festival or on a gala day when they brought in a whale. I saw native dancing, but it was exhibition dancing, not celebration dancing. Still, I did get a glimpse of children who were alive to their own world and to what might lie beyond. One fifth-grade girl with whom I made instant friends brought me a gift as I was leaving — a four-inch piece of old yellowed walrus ivory carved into two rows of teeth. It had been dug up, she explained. Someone long, long ago had tied this piece of ivory to the bottom of his shoe so he could walk on ice without slipping. Ancient, land-bridge cleats. "Are you sure you want to *give* this to me?" I asked. She was sure. "But this isn't a present," I told her. "It's magic." Her eyes were shining . . . "I know," she said, and I think she did know. She was giving me a piece of the Unknown from her world, a talisman to take back to my world, which I knew from her many questions seemed farther removed to her than the land bridge.

I would have liked to have spent more time with this girl and indeed with all the children I met. Instead, I left books behind. Whether they will be read, I don't know. You never know. I don't write for schools, yet I would be disappointed if schools didn't make use of them. But of course, I am frustrated at the limitations of books. No book ever lives up to a writer's original vision of it. What I would really like to do is to line up with all my tribesmen in the educational and book business and shake gourds to wake up those out there who may be nodding off. "We're alive!" I want to say. Instead, I take a slow, devious route, but it is the one which seems to serve me. My excursions into history are my way of saying, "We're alive and we always have been." The past really *was*, and when we are convinced of this, when we take possession of it, our present is invigorated.

How do we enter the past? One of my favorite nonfiction books is a book on natural science. Although it describes the process of entering the secret world of living creatures — animals, insects, birds — the process can also apply to human beings and to the secret worlds they have left behind. The book is *The View from the Oak* by Judith and Herbert Kohl. They quote from a theoretical biologist. "We now know," he writes, "that there is not one space and one time only, but there are as many spaces and times as there are subjects, as each subject is contained by its own environment which possesses its own space and time." He uses the word *Umvelt* to embrace the world and the organized experience that is special to each creature. "To become close to other worlds," he says, "means giving up our own for a while."[2]

Well, we do have to give up our own world temporarily in order to travel backward. It is a matter of housecleaning, ridding our minds of food, ready-made soap, telephones, but I suggest that if we stop there, the process can be self-defeating. When we give children projects in making soap and candles, dress them up in period costume, we may be transporting them back in time, but it's an excursion trip. A preliminary exercise. More often than not, the child returns with the idea that the past was primarily quaint. A young girl wrote me recently: "I would love to have lived long ago and churned butter on a nice neat little prairie." The expression "long ago" in itself may be a danger sign. When children use it, it is apt to have a sentimental, nostalgic, simplistic ring to it. I tend to stick to the word *past* and I'm not out to make that past seem uncomfortable — just more strenuous and complicated than anything that might take place on a neat little prairie. Also, I want to make clear that the same old emotions that we live with today — they were all back there, just plugged into different outlets, connected to different circumstances.

How do we do this? How do I, for instance, decide how

much a character of mine is responsible for his own actions? How much is decided by his times? Was I fair to represent King George as a well-meaning but very obtuse man? The keeper of the queen's archives, who had written extensively about King George, didn't think so. When I interviewed him in London, he defended George the Third strongly against what I suspect he thought was my American prejudice. "He was a product of his times," he argued. "How could he have done differently?" He overlooked the fact that there were those in England and in Parliament who did understand the colonies. Indeed, there would never have been arguments in Parliament if the policy toward the colonies had not been open to choice, subject to debate. It seems to me that George the Third was less conditioned by his times than he was by his own rigid temperament, a rigidity he expressed in every area of his life twenty-four hours of the day. From his point of view, his life was sad and I am sympathetic; yet, with two hundred years between us, I can also afford to find him funny. And I do.

George the Third is still somewhat of a sensitive subject in England. And of course, when I'm writing about our country, I am continually running into such subjects. How can I write about the eighteenth century, for instance, without dealing with slavery? Yet, there will be criticism. On the one hand, a textbook company did not want me to remind anyone that slavery ever existed. No, they said, I could not state that Patrick Henry received slaves as a wedding gift. On the other hand, at a children's literature conference, I was challenged to tell children that Washington and Jefferson were hypocrites who claimed to oppose slavery but did not free their own slaves. As a matter of fact, Washington did free his slaves at his death, all but the few who were to take care of Martha. Of course, some of his slaves had to grow old as slaves before he died. But if I truly enter the eighteenth century, how can I either excuse or blame these men? I certainly don't have to abandon my twentieth-century convictions or my pain and anger over the fact that the institution of slavery existed, but still, I have to face the complexity of the issue that in the 1700s was tied so inexorably to the unity of the young republic. But yes, the Founding Fathers' concept of liberty, so revolutionary in some ways, was limited — one might say warped — in others. They might deplore slavery, but neither Madison nor Jefferson, for example, could imagine a society composed of free blacks and whites living side by side. The best solution they could come up with was a colony for freed slaves in the American West or in Africa, which was no solution at all. So, in my book on James Madison, I was delighted to report that Dolley Madison's father had the moral fortitude to free his slaves, to give up his plantation, and to move north. I was equally sad to report that he didn't make it in the north.

A writer of history has to assimilate the psychology of both the times and the specific character. This is a slow process. Your character comes into focus gradually as you piece together fragments of time and see, sometimes in a flash, how one set of circumstances plays into the next. But in order to make connections, a biographer's imagination has to be at work. Van Wyck Brooks says: "All of a biographer's facts are useless until he has reconceived them in the light of his intuitive feelings for reality and proportion." Consider the year just prior to James Madison's wedding. There is a confluence of events that by themselves do not seem to lead anywhere. But add them up and see what we have. We know that in the fall of 1792, Madison's favorite brother, Ambrose, died. We find out his father's health was failing. We remember that Jefferson, Madison's best friend, had given notice that he would leave the government at the end of the year. And we understand that Madison was no longer on the same close terms with Washington as he had been. Madison himself did not add up all these discouraging aspects of his life, but his letters are downhearted. Of course, he felt lonely, and of course, any sympathetic reader would wish he had a companion to cheer him up. And before long, there is Dolley Payne Todd, newly widowed, pretty as a picture. Her arrival on stage was partly by chance (and a biographer should never underestimate chance), but surely it was also because James was ready for her. So, as a biographer who is telling a story, I gather up the known facts to prepare Madison as well as the reader for what lies ahead.

Timing is important. Just because the action takes place in a known past is no excuse for depriving the reader of a sense of that Unknown which is part of every life, no matter when it is lived. Biographers must preserve a sense of immediacy and proceed into the futures of their characters' lives as fiction writers do, as if this were unexplored territory. The reader knows at the outset that James Madison was the fourth president of the United States, but the biographer should create enough tension, enough suspense, enough involvement so that piece of knowledge does not reduce the readers' curiosity. How did Madison become president? Why? How did he feel? Where the facts permit, the biographer, again like the fiction writer, plants hints that foreshadow what is coming. In the life of Theodore Roosevelt that I have just finished writing, there was no lack of such ready-made hints. Long before Roosevelt entered national politics, newspaper writers were speculating that one day he might make it to the White House. Roosevelt himself admitted that he entertained such daydreams.

In some ways, historians have the advantage over fiction writers. They can permit surprises to occur, no matter how incredible. They can let coincidences take place, however farfetched, as long as they are documented. Novelists, on the other hand, are wary of introducing anything that suggests easy, contrived solutions. If they let something as wayward as weather, for instance, determine the outcome of a plot, who would believe them? Yet, I have been amazed at how often freaky weather has turned the tide of American history. Would the progress of the Revolutionary War have been changed on March 5, 1776, if a violent storm had not come up just as General Howe was embarking from Boston to fight the Americans at Dorchester? As it turned out, he never did go to Dorchester. While waiting for the storm to subside, General Howe changed his mind. The next day, he evacuated Boston and sailed for New York. Again — would the burning of Washington in the War of 1812 have been prolonged if a hurricane had not hit Washington the morning after the British entered it? This was no ordinary hurricane but one of such mammoth proportions that the British ran for their lives. I loved describing this scene in my book. But if I had been writing fiction, I would never have had the nerve to create such a horrendous hurricane.

Actually, fighting battles is not my favorite occupation.

Yet, once I master the flank movements, once I am able to reduce the action to something I can visualize, I fall under the spell of the drama. Characters reveal themselves; emotions run strong; luck as well as strategy takes the day. The most heartbreaking battle I've fought was the Battle of Fredericksburg in the Civil War. Oh, I hated to send those Union soldiers relentlessly, line after line, across that empty field to certain death. It was not weather that determined the outcome of this battle, but the stubbornness of General Burnside, who had promised to get his men to Richmond through Fredericksburg, and he meant to keep his promise, whatever the cost. Still, natural elements did add rare and unexpected drama to the story. The night after the battle, when the Union soldiers were burying the dead, a brilliant display of Northern Lights suddenly filled the sky. For Northern Lights to appear in Virginia was extraordinary in itself. But for them to appear that night in those tragic circumstances! It was as if Heaven itself were moved to provide a ceremony for that grim burial. No storyteller, however, no matter how tempted, would dare make up such a finale. Yet, for the historian, there it is, ready for the taking.

I suspect that there are far more surprises lurking in the crannies of history than anyone supposes. Sometimes I sniff something that smells suspiciously like a surprise. I put my nose to the ground and take up the chase. All for nothing. So it was when, in the course of writing about Benedict Arnold, I met one John Brown, who hated Arnold with a passion that was overpowering. He had obvious reasons. He was with Ethan Allen at Ticonderoga when Benedict Arnold arrived and with his usual arrogance tried to take command. Brown served with Arnold in Canada when smallpox broke out in the camp and Arnold ordered wholesale inoculation. This was a fairly new procedure and still hotly contested, and when Brown's brother died, Brown held Arnold personally responsible. Then, when Arnold denied John Brown a promotion on the ground that Brown had stolen from the enemy's baggage carts, Brown became obsessed with the need for revenge. He went to the Continental Congress, from "general to general," he said, recounting the instances of Arnold's misconduct. When no one paid any attention, Brown resigned from the service. In frustration he posted a public notice in Albany, listing his grievances against Arnold and ending with the charge, "Money is this man's god, and to get enough of it, he would sacrifice his country." This was long before Arnold had even thought of defecting. He was still a hero, celebrated for his bravery, so this was an extravagant accusation.

Money — that problem had not surfaced before. Yet, in order to make the charge, surely money lay at the root of Brown's hatred. Surely, there was something we didn't know. On looking further into Brown's life, I discovered that he was married to a cousin of Benedict Arnold. I found out that Arnold was known for borrowing from relatives, and was not particularly conscientious about paying them back. Had he borrowed from John's wife? Did John Brown's consuming anger stem from a family feud? I followed every clue I could find, both in his home community in Massachusetts and in New Haven, where he had once lived at the same time as Arnold had lived there. Nothing turned up. Had I been writing fiction, I could have invented a family motivation which my intuition tells me may have existed. I could have invented a smashing dialogue to vent the anger between the two men. I would have enjoyed that. But nonfiction writers do not have that option; they make do with what is on the record, and feel lucky to find as much as they do.

I did, however, wonder what John Brown said when he heard that Arnold had actually sold out his country. I looked up his whereabouts at the time. I wanted to hear him say, "I told you so." I longed to be present when he found out he was vindicated. John Brown was fighting Indians in upstate New York at the time of the West Point episode; he was killed before the news could have reached him. If the surprises of history are mind-boggling, so are the ironies. My only comfort is that I gave John Brown a larger role in my story than is generally given him by history.

If I were an academic historian, I might not be as excited as I am about the stories I find. Lytton Strachey says that ignorance is the first requisite of the historian. Only one who starts out ignorant, he claims, is able to select, simplify, omit. On this score Strachey would have to admit that I am well qualified to write. Although I have taken many history courses, none of them brought the past to life for me, so in a real sense, I started from scratch. For me, the great joy of writing biography is that I am learning at the same time as I am passing on what I have learned. If I make the material sound fresh, it is because it is fresh to me. I am still marveling over the very deliberate way so many of my characters shaped their lives, most in an attempt to compensate for something gone wrong in their childhood. And, like Barbara Tuchman, I am struck by how often people, as well as societies, believe what they want to believe and act on these beliefs, no matter how self-destructive they may be, no matter if there are viable alternatives.

But here I am, sounding as if I view history as a way of teaching lessons, transmitting specific attitudes. I don't think I am guilty of intentional indoctrination, but still, I am who I am. I, too, am a product of my culture and my past, and this is something we have to assess as we read every writer of history. The very slant of history changes from century to century. In the eighteenth century, historians were apt to center their attention on the villains of history. Caesar, Napoleon, Cromwell — they were all testaments to the danger of power. Later, we put larger-than-life heroes on stage, expecting them to provide examples of good conduct. For a while, we went through a period of presenting American history to children as if it were a story lifted from Norman Rockwell — wholesome, middle-class, and white. The authors fictionalized, inventing dialogue, presumably because they thought that was the only way to catch the attention of young readers. What they were doing, however, was minimizing the capacity of children and underestimating the stuff of history. To make a character accessible, you do not transport him or her to the reader; you take the reader to the character.

More recently, we have been talking about role models, focusing on men and women of all races and nationalities whose lives can serve as an inspiration, especially to minority children, who had previously been overlooked in our literature. Well, I think all of these approaches — with the exception of the Norman Rockwell approach — have legitimacy. It's a good idea to present villains, as long as they are not simply the bad guys, born to be bad. And heroes. We need heroes, as long as they are not just the good guys on pedestals so high that we can't reach them. Role models — fine, although I don't like the term and worry that it may be taken too literally. We don't want history to be didactic, as it can so easily be, as it so often has been. When I was in China several years ago doing research for my book *China's Long March,* I was interviewed by two reporters from *People's Daily.* They were puzzled by my project. "Why," they asked, "do you want to write a book about the Long March for *American* children? Do you want America to take a Long March?" In other words, they could see no point in writing a book that did not have a direct application to the behavior of a child. I tried to explain: "I want American children to understand China," I said.

Where children's literature is concerned, the Chinese are, for the most part, about where we were in the days when Parson Weems was manufacturing his cherry tree story. Obviously, Parson Weems wanted to present Washington as a character for children to emulate. But how many children would find a Valley Forge in their lives? So he invented the famous "I cannot tell a lie" quote. The moral of the story, whether Parson Weems realized it or not, is that you can get away with almost anything as long as you "fess up." I doubt if children are taken in. They know that if they begin swinging hatchets, truth alone may not save them. And when they discover that the story is only a myth, they will surely be struck by the irony of a man who resorted to falsehood in order to preach honesty. I think we have abandoned such a didactic approach, but not entirely. I get mail from both teachers and children worried about the corruption in my books. Why did I show young Ben Franklin swimming in the nude? Why did I quote a British Officer saying, "Damn?" In my book on

Columbus, why did I let the natives run around without any clothes? What can I say? History can be shocking. We won't learn much if we start out rejecting a young boy's bare bottom.

I dote on small details. Seemingly unimportant, they are in a way the lifeblood of the past. In researching Franklin, I read in one book after another that once Franklin learned ten swimming tricks. What were they? The authors didn't specify; they left me hanging. After a long search, I finally tracked them down. I don't expect readers to try out the tricks. I doubt if many will cut their toenails under water, but surely, they'll be intrigued by young Franklin. Who knows what he might try next? Over the centuries, the most respected historians have valued explicity. When Lord Macauley was asked how he came to be a historian, he said it was because as a child he had been a daydreamer. Indeed, he still liked to build imaginary castles, but in order to build a castle, he had to know exactly what kind of stones to use and how to assemble them. When walking down a London street, he had the habit of imagining that he was in Rome, so of course, he needed to be familiar with the geography and the landmarks of Rome. How could he proceed if he didn't recognize the buildings? A small fact can sometimes break down the barriers of space and time in a single blow. Does it make a difference that George Washington started off for the Constitutional Convention with a stomachache? Or that Andrew Jackson fought the Battle of New Orleans while undergoing an acute attack of dysentery? No, of course not. But it brought me to their side in a flash. The homely undercurrents of history, parenthetical though they may be, do sometimes illuminate great moments.

I have talked about some of the different ways history

has been presented to children over the years, but there is one book that seems to defy classification. In 1922, Hendrik Van Loon's *The Story of Mankind* won the first Newbery Medal, and though I doubt if children today will read such a long, ambitious book, I think it should be honored. Yes, occasionally attitudes show up which are not in tune with our times. The book tends to be avuncular in tone, as books for children often were in that day. But Hendrik Van Loon makes such a charming uncle and has such a wry sense of humor, we welcome him whenever he makes a personal appearance on his pages, offering philosophic observations, reminiscing about his own experiences. Although he covers the whole of mankind's history from evolution through World War I, he never fails to make his characters come alive, sometimes with only a sprinkling of choice words. He is not trying to present a comprehensive picture, and indeed how could he? His work is a voluminous feast, yet it is designed, he says, as an appetizer, to give children a taste for history. That's enough. Those of us who write about the past could not hope for more. In his opening sentences, Mr. Van Loon establishes, it seems to me, exactly the right tone.

"We live under the shadow of a gigantic question mark," he writes.

"Who are we?

"Where do we come from?

"Whither are we bound?"

Before proceeding to known facts, he spreads out the Unknown. Never does he lose touch with the mystery that lies at the root of knowledge; never does his enthusiasm flag or his wit flounder.

That enthusiasm is what historians and teachers of history need — a zest for story and an unquenchable curiosity about people. "The art of history remains always the art of narrative. That is the bedrock." So wrote G. M. Trevelyan. Unlike novelists, biographers cannot invent their facts, but they do have to understand and use the techniques of fiction. Herodotus said that past events, recounted in history, should never lose their radiance. We reach for radiance and for the spark that will bring people to life. Sometimes, when I am preparing a biography, I have the physical sensation that I am digging with my hands, scratching with my fingernails into the earth in the effort to rescue past lives. I once wrote an adult biography about an eighteenth-century lady, Mercy Otis Warren, whose portrait was painted by Copley — a stern, prim-looking woman with a tense mouth. I was drawn to her, but knew I couldn't write about her until I had seen her smile. I kept a small reproduction of her portrait on my desk and as I did my research I watched her closely, trying to catch her off guard. For a long time, she was adamant, but finally, she accommodated me. I caught the first glimpse of a smile in her eyes, and then it took hold and I was ready.

Nothing pleases me more than to hear from children who have made contact with my characters. "I can understand John Hancock," one boy wrote, "I'm a lot like him. I want everyone to like me, too." And from a girl who had read *Early Thunder:* "I understand Daniel's problem," she said. "I think it's hard to do what you think you should do when other people expect you to do differently." And there was a boy who came to the defense of Benedict Arnold. "I don't blame Benedict Arnold one bit," he wrote. "If I'd been with him in the aftermath of Saratoga, I would have done just what he did. I want you to know that there is one person in these United States of America who weeps for Benedict Arnold."

Well, I do blame him, but I weep, too. Who can read history without weeping? And without laughing. I hope that young people will see that history, like life itself, is filled with tragedy, comedy, farce, paradox, surprise, mystery, courage, and failure. And I speak for all of us, I think, when, using Annie Dillard's words, I say, our job is to keep children awake. We don't want them to miss the show.

NOTES

1. Jean Fritz, *And Then What Happened, Paul Revere?* (New York: Putnam, 1973).
2. Judith and Herbert Kohl, *The View from the Oak* (New York: Sierra Club Books/Scribner, 1977).

Introduction to Trina Schart Hyman

TRINA SCHART HYMAN was born for mischief. Fortunately, she can draw, and even though her drawings are sometimes mischievous, too, that has proved refreshing in a field where so many adults are trying to impress the proper values on mischievous children. Critics have not always appreciated Trina's visual sense of humor. Once, in response to a damning review in *Kirkus*, Trina drew, in her next book, an unobtrusive gravestone with an epitaph for Virginia Kirkus. The hue and cry over this bit of impropriety took years to die down. Meantime, Trina kept drawing. She drew wolves and children straying from the forest path, and her *Little Red Riding Hood* was a Caldecott Honor Book in 1984. She drew dragons and knights and won the Caldecott Award for *St. George and the Dragon*, adapted from Spenser's *Fairie Queene* by Margaret Hodges in 1985. She drew demons in a 1990 Caldecott Honor Book, *Hershel and the Hanukkah Goblins* by Eric Kimmel. Her versions of *Snow White, Sleeping Beauty,* and *Rapunzel* resonate with deep color, romantic style, and theatrical stage effects.

In addition to folk and fairy tales, she's illustrated an

astonishing range of children's literature, from how-to nonfiction and historical biography to poetry collections and contemporary novels. She has taken on Chaucer in a 1988 edition of *Canterbury Tales;* Sir Thomas Malory in *The Kitchen Knight;* Charles Dickens in *A Christmas Carol;* Mark Twain in *A Connecticut Yankee in King Arthur's Court;* J. M. Barrie in *Peter Pan;* and Dylan Thomas in *A Child's Christmas in Wales.*

Blessed with an ability to draw expressive portraits as well as anatomically graceful bodies, she has provoked reaction with seductive figures — always true to the characters portrayed — in *King Stork* (Howard Pyle) and *Two Queens of Heaven: Aphrodite and Demeter* (Doris Gates). Clearly one of the best draftspersons illustrating for children, she has deepened her artistry from the inventive swirl of lines that cast their spell in *Magic in the Mist* by Margaret Kimmel to the dramatic strength of *How Does It Feel to Be Old?* by Norma Farber.

With thirty-three books still in print, Trina has ventured into new directions of composition and design without losing her sense of proportion and perspective. To be meticulous as well as fanciful has been time-consuming, over the years, but she also once shaped the art direction of one of the best juvenile magazines in the country, *Cricket.* Now, in a competitive arena where artists are understandably opting for full royalties by writing picture books as well as illustrating them (with some very thin stories as a consequence), Trina just keeps drawing and painting, which results in books better worded by writers and best illustrated by herself.

Trina Schart Hyman is a story artist. She expands the imaginative possibilities of a tale, instead of limiting them by clichéd images. Her graphics lead fluidly to other thoughts and the exploration of other words. Every good illustration opens a reader's imagination to his or her own pictorial fantasies, a point missed by those who claim that fairy tales should not be illustrated for fear of curbing the child's inner vision. Rather, fairy tales should not be illustrated badly in ways that dull visual development.

I have a deep attachment to Trina, not only because she paints as vividly as I dream, but because, whenever we've met over the last two decades, we've been able to talk about the business of children's literature with a rare honesty that is not always reassuring, but is always stimulating. I can promise you more of the same. Trina Schart Hyman.

Trina Schart Hyman

Zen and the Art of Children's Book Illustration
May 3, 1991

I GUESS I SHOULD TRY to explain my choice of a title for this thing. I feel as though I have to defend myself, because when I told my daughter I was going to call it "Zen and the Art of Children's Book Illustration," she made gagging noises and said, "Oh God, you *didn't*! How embarrassing!" And when I told one of my colleagues, she just stared at me in silence for a few seconds and then murmured, "How original!"

So, let me explain.

Once upon a time, long ago in the 1950s, I was an illustration student in an art school in Philadelphia. These were among the happiest years of my life. That's because I was very young and unbelievably ignorant. In those days, it was always springtime, I was usually madly in love, the world was full of exciting possibilities, and I was under the impression it had all been arranged for my benefit. You know how it is.

Anyhow, one day in drawing class when the model was taking a break and we were all just standing around and shooting the breeze and smoking unfiltered cigarettes, the instructor told us a story about Leonardo da Vinci.

It seems that the pope wanted a big new fresco painted in the Vatican dining room or someplace like that, and in order to decide who should be awarded the commission, he asked for an open submission of sketches. Word was sent out through all of Europe that in six months' time on a certain day, there'd be a big shindig at the Vatican, and any artist interested in the fresco job should come and present his comprehensive sketch to the pope and the fresco committee for judging; may the best artist win. So all the Renaissance hotshots got busy at their respective drawing boards, because this was an extremely well-paid and prestigious commission. All except Leonardo, who was probably fooling around with an idea for a new flying machine.

Well, the big day arrived, and all the artists and everybody at the Vatican including the pope were standing around in the pope's reception room looking at the beautiful drawings and admiring them, when all of a sudden the door opens and in comes Leonardo. Not only late, but empty-handed as well. He goes right up to the pope and says, "You should give the fresco commission to me, because I am the best artist in this room."

"But Leonardo," said the pope (not unreasonably), "how can we know that you're the best artist if you didn't bring a sketch? How can we judge your abilities?"

"I don't need a sketch to prove to you what my hands and eyes are capable of," answered Leonardo, and thereupon, he asked one of the monks to bring him a good-sized brush and pot of ink. And there, right on the floor of the Vatican, right at the pope's feet, he drew — freehand, in one sure, swift, continuous motion — a perfect circle! Needless to say, he got the job.

It's a good story, and we were all impressed by it. Except I guess I wasn't impressed in the right way, because I opened my big mouth and the words that came out were, "I could do that." My drawing teacher just looked at me. He said, "You think you could do that? I'll bet you five dollars you can't." And he handed me a stick of black conté crayon. "Go ahead — I dare you!"

Now, I didn't have five dollars. I had about forty-two cents and three subway tokens to last me until the end of the week. But I did have plenty of chutzpah. As I mentioned, I was young and ignorant. So I took the conté crayon, and didn't dare think about the five dollars or about making a fool of myself or anything like that. I just thought *perfect circle* and then I drew one on the floor. I did it! And if it wasn't exactly, precisely perfect, it was near enough when the instructor checked it out with a compass. He gave me the five bucks, too! Then he asked me, "How did you *do* that?"

At the time, I had no idea how I did it. I knew I was no Leonardo da Vinci; I may have been young and ignorant, but I wasn't stupid. I might have thought that the hand of Leonardo came down from the sky and guided mine because he knew I needed the five dollars. And I did know that my drawing instructor and my classmates were thinking *beginner's luck* or else *smart-alecky little bitch*.

Okay. Let's fast-forward in time a bit. I know this is a long explanation for a stupid title, but bear with me.

Eighteen years later, I told this story to a good friend of mine, who also happened to be the editor of a book I was working on. It was, I believe, the very first book in which I thought of using decorative borders as a device to frame the page. It was called *Meet Guguze,* a translation of charming little stories about a kid named Guguze. Since they were by a Russian writer, I went for inspiration to the only Russian illustrator I was aware of, Ivan Bilibin, who used decorative borders to frame his illustrations the way most people use adjectives in their everyday speech, only better.

Anyhow, when you're going to frame anything, at some point you have to use straight lines. The way I do it is to draw a faint line in pencil with a ruler, and then use a brush and ink — freehand — to follow the pencil line.

My friend the editor was watching over my shoulder as I was doing one of these freehand ink lines, and she said, "How do you *do* that?" And I said, "You just saw me. I draw a line with a pencil and ruler and then — " And she said, "No, no. Anybody can draw a straight line with a ruler. But you just follow it down with your brush, without the ruler, and it comes out straight! How do you *do* that?" I said I couldn't always do it without a goof or a wobble, and then all of a sudden, I remembered my art school drawing class and the story about Leonardo, and I told her — a little smugly, I admit — about my five-dollar triumph. "I'm going to send you a book I think you should read," she said.

The book was *Zen in the Art of Archery* by Eugen Herrigel. It's a little piece of autobiography about a German guy who goes to Japan to find out about Zen and to learn the ancient art of archery at the same time. He studies under one of the great masters of Zen and archery, and what he finds out after three years is basically this: To shoot an arrow perfectly straight and true, with grace and precision and beauty and ease, so that it hits the target smack on, what you have to do is forget about the bow,

forget about the arrow, forget about the technique of raising the bow, drawing the bowstring, loosing the arrow.
Forget about yourself, the weather, the outside world, or
any thought of how to hit the target. What you have to do
is become the arrow, become the path of the arrow toward
its goal, become the target, and never ever be conscious of
the actions involved in any of this. Learn the technique,
and then forget it completely. Lose yourself, stop thinking,
become the arrow, and you will hit your target.

But this doesn't only apply to archery, you see. Lose
yourself, become the brush, become the line, think only of
the stopping point, that is, the goal, and you will draw a
straight line. Or a perfect circle.

Now, don't get me wrong. Obviously, I'm not Ed Young
— I mean, he is really a Zen kind of person; his work
shows it. I'm a baby at this Zen business. I can only use it
occasionally and awkwardly. I'm too much a creature of
the West, with a Westerner's jittery ego, to be successful
at any kind of concentrative meditative technique.

However, this little book had a profound effect on me.
It didn't exactly change my life, but it answered some
questions for me, and it gave me a sort of tool — an approach, as it were — that I think I already had an aptitude
for. That's where my perfect circle came from, I think. It's
an approach I've been able to use quite often in my work
as an illustrator.

For instance, when I was drawing all those quadruple-
red-cross borders for *Saint George and the Dragon*, that
was a whole lot of freehand straight lines, believe me: 256
of them, to be exact. And I couldn't let myself mess up or
let them go wobbly, because I was working on the sort of
paper surface that doesn't take kindly to the usual ink-

erasing devices, like scratching out with a razor blade or covering up with white-out. This same temperamental surface also happens to give you a kind of burn when your drawing hand moves across it; it hurts just enough so that your stomach gets a tiny bit queasy. On top of all this, I have wonky eyes. One of the problems with them is reduced depth perception, which manifests itself in seeing double image, especially when I've strained the muscles a lot. When I look at a straight line close up, after a few seconds it becomes two parallel lines. Fun, when you're inking borders.

On top of everything — trying to cope with a burning hand, a queasy stomach, and two lines where there should be one — imagine that the telephone rings. Or the dogs start barking. Or the electricity goes off. In other words, the outside world interferes. This is where Zen comes in very handy. I shut off my physical self and everything else in the world. The only thing that exists is the line. I become the line. It works! It never gets easier to do, but at least it becomes more familiar.

I slowly came to realize that I had always used this kind of zoning-out-to-tune-in with other aspects of my work. For instance, the whole problem of developing and visually maintaining a character throughout a book was always easy for me, as long as I knew who that character was. If ever I had any doubt about who that peasant boy, or knight, or princess, or dwarf should be — if I couldn't visualize them and put my whole conscious and unconscious self in their place as I was working on the story — then the illustration was always in danger of falling apart. So I would "Zen myself out," and that way become the character.

If I want to know what a place feels like or what the sky looks like after a certain patch of weather, I search deep inside my memory to find it, then put everything aside and go there, and then I try to find the right lines and colors to put it down. If I don't know about the place, person, or thing — that is, if I haven't experienced it personally — then I try to find out about it. For example, when it became clear at a certain point that I knew almost nothing about horses except that I liked to look at them, I decided to sign up for lessons at a nearby stable. I'm actually rather leery of horses on any intimate basis. Anything that big and powerful that operates solely on instinct and nerves and a tiny lentil brain is to be afraid of. But I took the lessons and stuck it out for a year, trying to "Zen out" the disdainful competence of several fearless ten-year-old fellow riders and the chillingly polite patience of the hatefully well-groomed and correct little yuppie Barbie doll who was our riding instructor.

I never really learned to ride well, but at least I learned something about horses. How they move, how they smell, and how it feels to be on horseback. I even came to like them. This is all extremely useful when I have to focus in on visualizing horses. Like the time I had to draw twenty-six of them, with riders, all moving across the title page spread of *The Canterbury Tales*. Or the time I had to draw St. George and his shire horse being picked up and carried through the air by a giant dragon.

Anyhow, this is how I came to use Zen — or something approximating Zen — in the art of illustrating children's books.

Now, I can hear a sensible, reasonable question forming in the back of some people's minds: "So, why bother with all this stuff? Why not just draw the stupid line with a ruler and a pen, if you want a straight line? Why not just find a picture of a horse or use photographs of people or set up a model? Why sweat it?"

The reason — for me — is that a straight line drawn with a ruling pen looks mechanical. It looks dead. It doesn't have that quality of human vulnerability that a hand-drawn and just slightly imperfect line will have.

"Yeah, but who would notice?" asks the sensible voice.

Well, I would notice. I also think that the feeling and look of the art would in some way be affected. *You* would notice, even if you didn't know exactly what you were seeing that was ever-so-slightly not there. I think the same thing, only much worse, happens when an artist works directly from photographs.

I'm not talking about using photographs for reference. I do that; every illustrator does. If you're not sure what happens when an arm is angled a certain way, or what makes a pinto pony different from an Appaloosa, or how the Chicago skyline looks, or a hawthorn tree, you go find a picture of the thing and you find out. What I'm talking about is setting up models in the poses you want for your illustration, taking a Polaroid shot, and working directly from the photograph — whether it's of the skyline, or the pinto pony, or the hawthorn tree, or the main character in the story. The photograph is either copied from directly, or an overhead projector flashes it onto your work surface and it's copied that way. That's how it's done.

A whole lot of illustrators work this way. It can be done very creatively, and it's certainly nothing new; Norman Rockwell, Maxfield Parrish, and countless other illustrators for magazines worked from photographs all the time.

But today, it's become much more common in illustrations for children's books than ever before.

Personally, I hate these illustrations. I hate them because no matter how technically sound or talented the illustrator may be, the result looks cold and mechanical and dead. Part of the reason for this may be that a photograph tends to diminish or even kill action or emotion simply by freezing it. You're not getting the essence of the gesture, you're getting a frozen millisecond of a piece of it, and a piece that is then artificially translated onto paper as well. I hate the slickness of this sort of work, the detachedness of it. It leaves no room for the grand gesture, the excitement or mystery or just plain humanity of direct contact between the story, the artist, the picture, and the reader.

The art in so many children's books lately seems to be concerned only with how it *looks* — with how stunning and well done and clever it is. There's not very much concern with conveying a feeling, a point of view, a sense of humor or of time or place, or even straightforward information about the story. It's all technique and no substance.

And what's really disturbing to me is that nobody seems to realize this has happened. If they do realize it, they don't care. Or maybe they like it. Anyway, it seems to be the current trend.

It's a very trendy business these days, making children's books. Just like our big cities, environmental issues, the television industry, and almost anything you can think of, the whole business seems to be basically out of control. Come to think of it, children's book publishing reminds me a lot of Cinderella, in more ways than one.

Now, Cinderella was a nice girl; she had a heart of gold

and she was cute as a button. But the poor kid got a raw deal when her father remarried. She was pushed into a corner, ignored, ridiculed, overworked, underpaid, and generally made to feel like doo-doo by her stepmother and stepsisters. But all of a sudden, the fairy godmother shows up. Cinderella gets some great-looking clothes and a fancy car and her big chance to catch an executive-type guy with money. Because she looks so terrific in her designer gown at the ball, the prince falls in love with her, finds out who she is, and marries her. Great. I wish them both luck.

Do you think for one minute that if she'd walked to the castle or even taken a bus, sneaked past the doormen, and then circulated among the guests in her raggedy old clothes and bare feet — do you think for even one minute that the prince would have noticed what a basically beautiful person she was? Get real.

My dear friend and best-loved publisher, John Briggs of Holiday House, has been after me for fifteen years to illustrate "Cinderella." So far, I've been able to put him off with *Little Red Riding Hood* and *Rapunzel* and a bunch of other projects. I don't have the heart to tell him straight out that I don't like the Cinderella story much. I don't like it because it's about sisters being mean to each other, but also because it's about the importance of pretty clothes. It's not about how things are, it's about how things look.

Children's books have a lot in common with Cinderella these days. For years, they've been pushed around, snickered at, underrated, overworked, and underpaid. But now they have a rich prince and some pretty clothes. Maybe it's happily ever after and maybe it isn't. But the marriage makes me nervous, if that's all it's based on.

Please understand that I'm speaking only from an illustrator's point of view. In my thirty years in the world of children's books, I've tried never to forget my place — the artist's place — which is usually a rather peculiar mixture of behind-the-scenes technician and star performer. I wouldn't presume — or want — to know what's going on with the authors, or the editorial side of things, or with the reviewers, or about the corporate takeovers. But during thirty years, many elements that should have nothing to do with illustrating books start to filter through. By now, they have come through with a vengeance. And the sad part is that I feel those things are affecting my work. I'm not sure what to do about it. It's hard to "Zen them out."

Books became big business, probably in the seventies and eighties when those major corporations whose executives had never read a book in their lives bought up most of the publishing houses. Ever since then, a lot of changes have taken place. And these changes have affected children's books in a profound way. You see, a book is not just a book anymore; it's a product. It's even called that — "the product." A product is expected to sell; it has to have lots of consumer appeal. The marketing strategy must be very well planned; rock stars, royalty, any big names connected with a product mean good things for sales. The product should also fit in with current social and economic trends — the hot topic, in other words. And by all means it must be well packaged; who cares if the quality is good — it should just look gorgeous!

Children's books used to be put together by an author, an editor, an illustrator, and maybe an art director. Some still are, but not many. "The product" is now planned by committee. The committee is comprised mostly of marketing people, maybe an editor or two, and maybe somebody from the art department. They develop the product with one eye on current fads and the other eye on the cash register.

(There's a cartoon in a recent issue of *The New Yorker*. A bunch of elegantly dressed middle-aged people are standing around at a cocktail party, and one of them is saying, "My latest book is for three- to five-year-olds, but I like to think there's something in it for everyone." It's funny, and true of course, but what's interesting to me is that this is now *New Yorker* material. See how trendy we are in children's publishing these days?)

I wonder, often, what the focus on this product really is. I somehow doubt that it's kids. I mean, let's be honest. It's not big news that children's books aren't produced for children. Children don't buy books. Children don't review books. Most children can't even read, and many of them don't even like to read. Of course, this has always been true. But in my early years of publishing, there was a different feel to it, even if the children themselves were not uppermost in the publishers' minds. Nobody expected children's books to make money in those days. It was an accepted fact — almost an honored tradition, even — that they didn't. And because they weren't expected to make money, you could just relax and do your thing. You could be a little weird if you wanted to, or silly, or simply sincere. You could even think about what might appeal to children. There wasn't all this emphasis on gorgeousness and trends and marketability. You could be gorgeous, of course; but it wasn't expected.

Being gorgeous was also more difficult to arrange. Most books in those days were illustrated in black-and-white or limited color, because there just wasn't a lot of money to spend on production. I had been illustrating professionally for thirteen years before I was allowed to do my first full-color book for a trade publisher. It was *Snow White.*

I don't regret or resent all those years of working when children's publishing meant the editor and you and the book, when children's publishing was the poor second cousin to adult trade publishing — "poor" in every sense. I feel lucky to have had those years. The discipline of working in black-and-white was great. It was actually freeing. Black-and-white sharpens your drawing and page-design skills and your creative imagination. I'm convinced some of my best books are the black-and-white ones, and I miss doing them. But hey — black-and-white doesn't suit the image we want our product to convey anymore. It's just not gorgeous enough; it wouldn't sell. But think about that committee that decides the fall list of books. Can you imagine that they'd ever consider Wanda Gág's *Millions of Cats?* Give me a break. Would you send Cinderella to the ball dressed in her *schmatte?*

Well, I'm sure you've heard it all before — today's emphasis on marketing, ideas-by-committee, and the "bottom line."

Listen. Just recently an editor called me up. He'd seen a copy of a book I'd done years ago for another publisher that's been long out of print. It's called *A Little Alphabet,* and it's my one and only attempt at an alphabet book. There's nothing impressive about it. It's a quiet little book that I did basically for my own amusement, and because I thought very young kids might like it. It's tiny — just big enough for a two-year-old's hands — and it's in black-and-white. The original publisher took it out of print after a while because (A) it was little, and small-trim-sized books are "definitely out"; and (B) it was in black-and-white, so it didn't sell. The editor who called me wants to republish it because (A) small-trim-sized books are "in" these days; but (B) black-and-white books still just don't sell, so he wants me to "colorize" it. Am I going to do it? Sure I am. Did Cinderella want to go to the ball?

So, as you can see, treating children's books as products has created many changes in publishing. One result of these changes is new and I think very interesting.

Children's book illustrations have suddenly become "collectible art." In the past few years, galleries have sprung up that sell only these original illustrations. And, as if sniffing out a trend, many public and private museums want to sponsor whole shows of children's art. This is all very seductive and flattering to children's book illustrators, most of whom have been living in the nether world of the arts for their professional lifetimes.

It's not exactly surprising that this is happening, given the stuff that's been churned out by the so-called fine-arts scene in recent years. It's a closed world. What we call today's fine art has become increasingly intellectualized into a secret language that most of us can't understand — except for that select group of people who are talking only to each other and to themselves. It has nothing to do with images that we can recognize.

People need images; it's a very basic human need. It's part of how we connect to our culture, our spirituality, even to our mythology. TV and the movies can't fulfill that need because their images leave no room for contemplation. Sometimes, we need to look quietly at a picture and feel a connection. That connection can be deeply personal and complicated, or it can be as simple as "I know that place, I recognize those people, and the sky looks like when. . . ." Or "Why does that guy look so terrified?" Or even, "Doesn't she remind you of Aunt Edith?"

Pictures we can connect to have disappeared from contemporary life. Illustration has mostly vanished from magazines and all advertising. Adult books stopped being illustrated sometime after the First World War. Today's adult book jackets rely mostly on typographic design with perhaps a discreet touch of photo-realist illustration; paperbacks use lots of embossing and "special effects."

Where are the pictures, then — the storytelling pictures that use images we can recognize? They are always to be found in children's books. And sometimes, they're even rather beautiful. So, it's not surprising to me that people should want to buy them to hang on their walls, and that galleries are springing up to sell them.

It's a good thing; all of it is good. But at the same time, it's doing something weird to my head, and also my work. Because now, all of a sudden, the implication is that you're not just illustrating a book — you're also potentially creating "pieces of art" that might be sold as paintings. I actually had a gallery owner tell me, "The clients love the art, but they all complain about those 'holes' in the picture — those spaces you leave for the text." I heard myself reply rather stiffly, "That 'hole' is the whole reason for the picture, you know." But nevertheless, I felt vaguely guilty. The seed of doubt and insecurity had been planted. I mean, shouldn't I have been able to do a great-looking piece of art for the picture book without, somehow, leaving that "hole" for the text? Should I be one of those illustrators who refuses to incorporate the text with the art? It all stays there, festering, in the back of my mind as I work. It drives me crazy when I'm designing a book. Like, what does a *real* artist do with that nasty little bit of type that gets in the way of the picture?

For all the years I've been in the business, I've heard children's-book illustrators telling each other and anyone else who would listen that illustration is just as good as — or just the same as — fine art. My own voice was just as loud as any in the chorus. Partly because I wanted to believe it, and also because there are so many instances where the two do overlap: Goya's etchings of the horrors of war; Daumier's drawings; Rembrandt's illustrations for the Bible. And among illustrators whose work is considered fine art are the early Florentines, and John Sloan, Gustave Doré, and Ben Shahn, among many others. The lines of distinction, especially in Western art before the last century, are very fuzzy. But I'm talking about right here and now.

Can illustration — children's book illustration in particular — be considered fine art? No, I don't think so. And I'll tell you why.

The fine artist is supposed to be concerned only with a spiritual or emotional expression that is purely his or her own. Fine art itself is concerned with — for lack of a more precise word — truth. For example, if you're painting a bowl of apples, you're trying to show what you personally feel about that bowl filled with apples; what makes it beautiful, unique, special to you. What makes it interest you, seduce you, entice you. What's happening as you see this bowl, those apples, and the space they're filling up? How do you perceive it? You don't care what anyone else is supposed to feel or perceive. You're not concerned with anything except with what you're seeing and how you see it. It's a private thing between you, the bowl of apples, and the painting you're working on. If your perception connects with someone else's, fine; if not, it doesn't matter a bit. You're trying to find out, in visual terms, the truth.

Illustration, on the other hand, can be concerned with personal expression only in a very indirect, third-hand kind of way through the story. And it is not at all concerned with truth. The purpose of illustration is to embellish, embroider, or amplify the text. It is necessary to exaggerate — to lie a little — to do this. That's why those photograph copiers, admirable though their technique may be, are not involving or connecting. To convey the feeling, the mood, the essence of a story — to involve the reader — it is necessary to use charm, wit, guile, and occasionally, the grand gesture. When illustrating for children, it is also necessary sometimes to put clothing on animals, to hide or disguise perfectly beautiful and useful parts of the human body, and to gloss over, prettify, or ignore many aspects of life in this real world. Those aspects that we, in our wisdom, deem unfit or unhealthy for the eyes of children. Lies; all lies.

Illustrators are artists who necessarily must lose touch with reality and who can only find truth of expression within the confines of telling a story to an audience. Illustrators are artists who have to use just that bit of artifice, theatricality, or charm to capture the reader and satisfy the client. I don't think this is bad — I wouldn't be here trying to stumble through this lecture if I did — but I don't think it's art.

Don't get me wrong. It's not at all my intention to criticize or complain about the buying and selling of original children's-book art. I think it's marvelous. I'd much rather that my illustrations be displayed on someone's wall than gather dust in a publisher's warehouse, be filed away in an archive somewhere, or rot in my own back pantry. But neither do I want to be seduced into thinking that I'm creating illustrations solely for the purpose of making pictures suitable for framing.

And in all that plethora of books, we're getting a whole lot of humbug. I'm not talking about the inconsequential popular numbskull stuff that has always been around, the stuff that plagues the people who are serious about children's literature and amuses their kids. I'm not talking about Rainbow Bears or Mutant Ninja Fairies or Walt Disney (are we laughing?) spinoffs, or titles like "Can Barbie and Ken Deal with Heterosexuality?" This kind of silly stuff has always been with us, and we put up with it because it serves a purpose. Kids need it because everybody needs a junk book once in a while; we need it, too, so we feel superior and have something to trash. What I'm talking about is self-consciously gorgeous humbug. Books that you look at and think, "Wow, this is so beautiful, it's just a work of art, I must buy it." So you spend sixteen dollars and then you get it home or in the library and the kids won't read it or look at it or listen to it more than once, and you sure as hell don't want to read it again, so what do you do with it? Put it on the shelf for posterity? Recycle it?

Who are these books being published for, anyway? They're not for children, obviously. They're not straightforward or unself-conscious or honest enough for that. Mostly, they're not interesting enough. They're not for grownups, either. When I want to read a book, I'll buy the latest John le Carré. When I want to look at art, I want Rembrandt or Monet or Gustave Caillebotte. If I want to see *Swan Lake,* I'll buy a ticket to the ballet.

So, who are we illustrators creating these books for? The galleries that want to sell the original art? The publishers who want to cash in on a trend? The marketing experts? Maybe we're working on becoming the new fine arts scene of the twenty-first century — maybe we're doing the same thing: talking to ourselves in a secret language, creating a product that is interesting only to its creator, reviewers, educators, and selected groupies. We, and the publishers, will just make our children's books so we can discuss them and write about them and admire them and sell them — often enough, to one another.

Let's go back to that art school in Philadelphia, back when our hearts were young and gay. Of the twenty-three people in my illustration class, only four of us had intentions of going into children's book illustration. The rest of the class thought we were crazy. The other three must've gotten sidetracked, because I've never come across their work anywhere. There was a guy in the class behind mine, however, named Jerry Pinkney. I guess he stuck it out.

In those long-ago days, children's books were sort of the low end of the totem pole. If you were going to be an illustrator, you wanted to illustrate stories in *Collier's, Esquire, Ladies' Home Journal, The Saturday Evening Post,* or that interesting new magazine called *Playboy.* You wanted to do record-album covers or go where the big bucks were, in advertising illustration. You know: grownup stuff. I chose children's books because I happen to love books. Also, I had — and still do have — a deep interest in mythology and folklore.

Most of the rest of my class wound up doing pasteups for graphic design studios or becoming art directors. Some drifted into the fine arts, and one of them had his paintings hanging in the Museum of Modern Art. As far as I know, I'm the only one who's been able to consistently earn my living doing what I love to do best — making pictures that tell a story.

I've been lucky, I tell myself. Children's books, rather than languishing or disappearing like the dinosaur, have grown and waxed healthy and sleek. Maybe too sleek. According to what I read in *Publishers Weekly*, it's where some mighty big bucks are.

So why am I complaining? What am I worried about? Why do I feel I've inadvertently gotten myself involved in something that's headed somewhere I never really wanted to go? Someplace where I feel uncomfortable, like I'd feel at Cinderella's ball? I don't know. Am I worried only about myself as an artist? Or about children's book illustration in general these days? I don't know that, either.

Maybe I should have called this talk "Zen and the Art of Aiming Carefully, and Then Shooting Yourself in the Foot."

Introduction to Betsy Byars

BETSY BYARS'S 1992 AUTOBIOGRAPHY, *The Moon and I,* is the best possible introduction to her work. She can no more resist telling a good story, even on herself, than fly. Actually, she flies, too, with the full credential of a pilot's license. Perhaps lifting over those clouds has contributed to a perspective that makes her one of the finest serio-comic writers in children's literature. Beginning with the Newbery Award for *The Summer of the Swans* in 1971, Betsy Byars has won enough awards, both critical and children's choice, to fill up columns of small print in several authors' biography series. Her fiction, book after book, has been included on the notable lists of major review journals and professional organizations, as well as on the programming of after-school television specials.

There's a clue to this success in one of Byars's recollections: "When I was young, I was mainly interested in having as much fun as possible." Somehow, she's kept that in mind for the children who comprise her audience. Byars's novels seem to reconcile that old polarity between the great literary works children won't read and the popular-appeal books so many of them cherish; here's a good writer whom children love to read.

Who among us, child or child-at-heart, could fail to identify with the likes of Mouse Farley in *The 18th Emergency,* the victim who must ultimately go forth alone and face his fate at a bully's hands? Marv Hammerman, the biggest boy in the sixth grade, is out to get Mouse for labeling him "Neanderthal Man," and we feel Mouse's agonizing suspense as he waits for vengeance to pounce. Comedy is tricky: too light, and it lacks substance; too dark, and it lacks balance. Try *The 18th Emergency* for substantial balance.

Byars is well known for her ability to render sad situations from a good-humored protagonist's perspective. *The Burning Questions of Bingo Brown* is a poignantly funny book about the first love between two classmates whose teacher is so smitten with an aerobics instructor that he attempts suicide after being rejected. Through classroom conversations and dynamics, which Bingo observes during his perpetual journeys to the pencil sharpener, readers gradually learn that it is the adult, rather than the preadolescent, who is losing control. Yet, neither is stereotyped, despite a prototypical middle-schooler "who had been in love three times in one day and had already had four mixed-sex conversations!" There's even a modicum of irony here, which is rare in humor for children. Bingo's nickname, applied because of the doctor's pronouncement upon delivering him, strikes Bingo as being more ludicrous than lucky. When a classroom drawing comes up, "Bingo knew his name would not be picked. He had never been chosen for anything in his life." In this event, he's proven wrong.

Byars has described her childhood as "uneventful." Reading one of her own accounts might even convince you to call her life "ordinary." Then you'll find yourself smiling at her extraordinary descriptions of an early hobby or perhaps, later, an obsession with boys. Here's an example of the hobby: "I was making my own clothes by the second grade, although I have a vague recollection of not being allowed to wear them out of the yard. I could make a gathered skirt in fifteen minutes. I sewed fast, without patterns, and with great hope and determination, and that is approximately the same way that I write." What she does in her writing is turn the ordinary inside out so that we see the inside seams — the quirks of what appear to be "average" people.

The first title in her Blossom series, *The Not-Just-Anybody Family,* could describe the distinctive characters in many of the thirty-four Byars books now in print, characters realized with such special effect that any reader who identifies with them feels suddenly a lot less like "just anybody." All this is rendered without a breath of didacticism; plot and dialogue do all the talking, from the beginning-to-read Golly sisters series through a versatile range of fiction including popular series books which can bridge that yawning gap between Francine Pascal and Rosemary Sutcliff. Whether she's handling contemporary metaphor with flair in *The Cartoonist* and *The TV Kid,* or dealing with problems of abuse and neglect in *The Pinballs* and *Cracker Jackson,* or juggling points of view among Blossom family members and their dog Mud, each narrative rings with a personal voice. Even in her series, more of the same is never quite the same.

For in vivid details lies Byars's greatest strength. Who else has described the writing process with such fresh perception as she does in her new autobiography? I myself have been sustained through several midnight deadlines by

Betsy Byars's description of writing a book: "Walk to re-
frigerator . . . 11 seconds. Take miniature Snickers from
freezer . . . 3 seconds. Warm Snicker in microwave . . . 16
seconds. Return eating Snicker . . . 11 seconds. Total
elapsed time . . . 41 seconds."

My personal favorite of all Betsy Byars's books is *The
Midnight Fox*. Lest I be charged with nostalgia, for it came
out in 1968 and was one of the first books I reviewed
during my first year as a professional reviewer, I reread it
this week, twenty-four years later, and found myself
moved once more both to laughter and to tears. I laughed
at Tom's imagining himself, on an unwelcome visit to a
farm, stampeded by two hundred chickens, "flattened on
the ground while the lead hen snatches the egg from my
crushed hand and returns in triumph to the coop." I cried
as Tom deals tragedy a sleight of hand by uncaging a
doomed fox. Experiencing those extreme emotions in such
close proximity is a sure sign that a reader is in Betsy Byars
country, roaming around in an imagination populated
with ordinary people whose individualistic traits and hard-
earned bits of wisdom make us see things in a different
way. Welcome tonight to Betsy Byars country.

Betsy Byars

Taking Humor Seriously
May 1, 1992

I EQUATE ZENA SUTHERLAND with humor. In the times — too few actually — we have been together, she has never once failed to make me laugh. Because of that, I chose my topic, and tonight I place this very classy lady in the company of some very classy gentlemen who have also made me laugh.

When my daughter was in second grade, she took me to school one day for "Show and Tell." This was the teacher's suggestion. She felt it would be beneficial for the kids to see what a real live author looked like. I went on, as I recall it, between some guppies and an interesting piece of fungus. And I hope you won't think I'm being immodest when I say I was the best.

I took a manuscript with me that day. I had just gotten it back, complete with editor's notes in the margin, and I showed the kids some of the editor's comments, one of which was "MAKE THIS FUNNY!" There was a great deal of interest in this demand, and the general consensus was that the editor meant for me to put some jokes in. If only it were so simple, for the truth is that there are far too many jokes in the world and far too little humor.

I once read that there are three ways to learn to write.

They are to write, to write, and to write. This is true, but I would add — certainly if the goal is to write humor — to read. I have always been drawn to humorous writing simply because I like to laugh and be amused. For years as I was growing up, the only thing I read in *The Saturday Evening Post* was the "Post Scripts" page. And while I was reading, by osmosis, I was absorbing certain facts about what is funny and why.

In Max Eastman's "Ten Commandments of the Comic Art," Commandment Three is "Be effortless." I especially like that, although there's a lot to be said for commandments five through eight — "Be plausible, Be sudden, Be neat, and Be right with your timing." But being effortless is almost my sole commandment, my goal in writing. I work on something until it looks as if I haven't worked on it at all, and if it looks as if I've worked on it, I go back and work some more. But it's especially important in humor. Humor demands naturalness and simplicity. To appear spontaneous may require a week of work. It's not like a James Thurber drawing that turned out funnier the faster he drew. More than any other type of writing, humor has got to resemble play.

Perhaps because they resembled play, humorous books attracted me as I was growing up. The titles of Leo Edwards's books drew me like a magnet — *Poppy Ott and the Prancing Pancake; Jerry Todd and the Purring Egg.* The books themselves rarely lived up to their titles, but they did make me realize that by manipulating language, you could be funny; by using an unusual adjective or adverb or description, you could intrigue a reader. *Jerry Todd and the Buffalo Bill Bathtub; Poppy Ott and the Stuttering Parrot; Jerry Todd and the Flying Flagdoodle.*

My uncle read the Cosmo Topper books, and I progressed to these. I must have read dozens of Thorne Smith's books during summer vacations when I was in high school. The Topper books, which have been ill-served by both the movies and TV with their emphasis on effects — cocktail shakers shaking in midair, tires changing themselves — are as fresh today as they were fifty years ago. They are very funny books, and Cosmo is a very funny man. The more familiar you become with him, the funnier he is, which may be the measurement of a truly humorous character.

One of the reasons the Topper books are so funny is that Cosmo takes himself seriously, just as Bingo Brown does in my books. They are earnest and straightforward. If Bingo and Cosmo thought they were funny, they wouldn't be. In my all-time favorite comic scene, Cosmo and the invisible Marion are sitting in a park. Cosmo reveals to Marion that as a boy he wanted to become an actor, and that the only encouragement he got was from a drunken uncle who gave him a book with photographs that showed you how to do Hate and Fear and Modesty and Surprise and practically all the other emotions. Unconsciously, Cosmo presses his hands to his cheeks and does Surprise for the invisible Marion, and he looks up to see a small group of bystanders, all of whom are registering the most eloquent surprise themselves, so that "Mr. Topper appeared to be leading a class in dramatic elocution."

I read a lot of Wodehouse too, and his young men also took themselves seriously. When love goes wrong, one of Wodehouse's characters plays "The Rosary" with one finger on the piano for hours. One can hardly be more serious than that.

I knew I owed a debt to both Thorne Smith and Wodehouse for the character of Bingo Brown, but I didn't realize the depth of my debt until I was rereading some of Wodehouse's books in preparing this talk. In my mind, Bingo had sprung into my head like a feat of magic. I had been working on a manuscript, and I needed a name for a character, and the name Bingo popped into mind. I liked it, but this was a minor character, and I didn't want to waste such an original name.

I tried to continue writing, but the character was beginning to form himself. Suddenly, I knew how he had gotten the name Bingo. When he was born, the doctor said, "Bingo!" I knew that later Bingo would say to his mom, "Mom, he wasn't naming me, he said that every time a baby was born." And pretty soon, I had to put aside the book I was working on and start writing about Bingo.

A name, a character wholly out of my imagination, I thought, and then I came across a Wodehouse short story called "No Wedding Bells for Bingo." Bingo Little is a minor comic character who appears frequently in Wodehouse stories. He is always becoming infatuated, and after seven ill-fated and very funny courtships, he falls in love with and marries the novelist Rosie M. Banks.

It doesn't always happen that I can trace a character or an incident directly to its source, but I know that while I was reading Wodehouse as a girl, Bingo Little entered my mind and emerged, as if from a cocoon, forty years later as Bingo Brown.

I am drawn to humor, but I am not a humorist. My own books are serious, with comic episodes. However, the humor is not what Mark Twain called "only a fragrance, a decoration." The humor in my books serves a dual purpose. It balances out the serious things. The more difficult the theme, the more humor is needed — for my own relief as well as the reader's. It also humanizes things that are so dreadful, they are in danger of dehumanizing us — wife abuse and child neglect, for example. The ability to laugh is the ability to put a distance between us, to give us the feeling that we're still in control.

The humorous parts of my books are my favorite parts. When I get one of my books and hold it in my hands for the first time, I open it immediately to the page with the Library of Congress summary. "A boy is puzzled by the comic and confusing questions of youth." This is helpful to me. Now when someone asks me what my new book is about, I am ready. "It's about a boy puzzled by the comic and confusing questions of youth."

After that, I leaf through the book, pausing at the parts I considered funny when I wrote them, to see if they have survived and are still funny in print.

Humor comes naturally to children. Max Eastman says that to children, "Every untoward, unprepared for, unmanageable, inauspicious, ugly, disgusting, puzzling, startling, deceiving, shaking, blinding, bolting, deafening, banging, bumping or otherwise shocking and disturbing thing, unless it be calamitous enough to force them out of the mood of play," is funny. He doesn't give the list for adults, but he does mention that it's a lot shorter.

The gap between what adults think is funny and what kids think is funny is considerable. Even Thurber says of children's humor, "There have been a great many times when I haven't the vaguest idea of what the hell they were laughing about." I know that there is a theory that we must never write *for* kids, not even humor, and if we even become aware that we are writing for kids, we've already lost the game, and after all, we're all just big kids, but I don't believe this. I refuse to think of myself as a large wrinkled child.

So, I'm always looking for things that are funny to kids. One of my daughters had some friends over one day, and one of the boys who was always comical noticed there were two cobwebs hanging from the ceiling. He got up on the piano bench and pretended to be Tarzan, attempting to swing from one to the other. It was very funny.

And so, in *The 18th Emergency*, when Mouse Fawley looks up on his ceiling and sees a cobweb, he doesn't try to swing on it, but he has previously written UNSAFE FOR PUBLIC SWINGING and drawn an arrow to it. This opened up a whole facet of Mouse's personality. When he sees a crack in the wall, he writes, TO OPEN BUILDING TEAR ALONG THIS LINE, and I would never have thought of that on my own.

My son had a friend who did whale imitations. I was never privileged to see them, because Phil never did his imitations on request but only when moved to do so. When this happened, the word would spread and kids would appear from blocks around to watch and roll on the floor, helpless with laughter. "What are the imitations like?" I asked my son. "They're like — whales," was his explanation. I sometimes found myself looking at Phil, the comic imitator of whales, wondering, but he looked back with his face in neutral, as all my son's friends did, and I could never imagine the imitations for myself. Years later, writing *Cracker Jackson*, with Jackson's friend Percy doing whale imitations, I did get a glimmer, and I can tell you the imitations were like — whales.

The forbidden is always funny, and usually the first kind of humor that kids discover is bathroom humor, and all too often, the appetite for this kind of humor is lifelong. At first, certain words are just plain hilarious, and the appeal of reducing one's friends to helpless laughter and, at the same time, shocking adults is considerable.

The funniest word in the vocabulary of a second-grader is *underwear*. When I speak to second-graders, I always read the opening sentence of *The Night Swimmers*. "When the swimming pool lights were turned out and Colonel and Mrs. Roberts had gone to bed, the Anderson kids came out of the bushes in their underwear." It is such a successful sentence with second-graders that I often have to repeat it. I have even been asked if I had any other funny sentences.

The difficulty with using bathroom humor, of course, is that it's hard to be tasteful. One of the ways is that you simply describe the joke rather than tell it. In *Cracker Jackson*, Goat had interrupted assembly by telling a joke during the Pledge of Allegiance. The principal calls Goat up and asks him to share "what was so funny" with the assembly.

I limit myself to: "The trouble was that the joke was about a man who had taken an overdose of laxative, and the principal couldn't shut Goat up before he gave the punch line, which consisted of a sound effect." That is too tasteful. Kids don't think that's funny.

I reached my peak as a bathroom humorist in *The 2000-Pound Goldfish*. The goldfish has been flushed down the toilet, into the sewer, where it comes to weigh two thousand pounds and has slurped five or six people to death. The soldiers are marching into the sewer to kill Bubbles, and Warren gets the idea that if everyone in the city flushed their toilets at, say, ten o'clock, the floodgates would open and Bubbles would be swept out to sea "where she could live the rest of her life in peace and harmony." This is the section I read aloud to kids, and at this point, some intellectual type raises his hand and says, "Mrs. Byars, goldfish can't live in salt water." I say, "Listen, I'm the boss of this book, and if I want Bubbles to live in salt water, Bubbles will live in salt water."

There follows a seven-page countdown in which the announcer is entreating listeners to flush their toilets. "It's five minutes to ten. If you have more than one bathroom, get a neighbor to come flush with you." "It's four minutes to ten, open your windows, yell, 'Flush!' to the people in the streets below." It takes two pages to get everyone in their bathrooms, and the final countdown is "Five-four-three-two-one-FLUSH!" and if I read this correctly, I never have to actually say the word *flush*, because the entire school will make the sound of a toilet flushing. It may not sound thrilling to you to hear two hundred kids flushing like toilets, but it has never failed to move me.

Bad grammar is more amusing to kids than good grammar although, increasingly these days, it seems no one knows the difference. The humor of bad grammar arose from the "bohunk" type of humor popular in early America. It was rural humor and the appeal was twofold — a feeling of superiority or gratified vanity that we ourselves knew better, and the enjoyment of irreverence and rebellion against the despised grammar book of youth. Even Mark Twain used it for humorous effect, and Artemus Ward made up a name for it, "ingrammaticisms," the thought being that as soon as you have learned that some grammatic form is "wrong," you are prepared to have fun with it.

My particular weakness has always been for the double negative. I am drawn to it. I am not sure I would have read and enjoyed H. Allen Smith's *How to Write Without Knowing Nothing* if the title had been, say, *How to Write Without a Great Deal of Education*.

Sometimes I use the double negative not to be funny, but to make the character's speech more authentic. In *Trouble River,* the grandmother says, "We ain't got no chance . . ." and "I didn't come no one thousand miles . . ." This was not meant to be funny, and it actually turned out to be unfunny, because I got letters from English teachers chastising me for reinforcing the unfortunate speech patterns which they were trying to change.

I've never quite come up to Robert J. Burdette, who, in "Romance of the Carpet," gained immortality with the quadruple negative, but then nobody has:

> And he turned away with a heart full sore,
> And he never was seen, not none no more.

Used properly, the double negative is funny. In *The 18th Emergency,* Mouse Fawley remembers when the boys decided, during a recess lull, to put the girls in the school trash cans. There's a long screaming charge, which ends with Mouse having Viola Angotti pinned against the garbage cans. He realizes he's not going to be able to get Viola in the garbage can without a great deal of help, but no help is forthcoming. Actually, the rest of the boys are being marched into the front door by the principal.

> He called again, "Come on, you guys, get the lid
> off this garbage can, will you?"

And then, when he said that, Viola Angotti had taken two steps forward. She said, "Nobody's putting me in no garbage can."

He cried, "Hey, you guys!" It was a plea. "Where are you?"

And then Viola Angotti had taken one more step, and with a faint sigh she had socked him in the stomach so hard that he had doubled over and lost his lunch.

As she walked past his body she said again, "Nobody's putting me in no garbage can." It had sounded like one of the world's basic truths. The sun will rise. The tides will flow. Nobody's putting Viola Angotti in no garbage can.[1]

Mark Twain said, "Repetition is a mighty power in the domain of humor," and James Thurber said that if "you keep on doing a thing, the audience will laugh," so it must be true. Repetition for fun is born early in a child's life, and who of us has not taken pleasure in the question, "Fuzzy Wuzzy wasn't fuzzy, was he?" Even in adulthood there's a certain pleasure in the fact that there was — and may still be — a newspaper called *The Walla-Walla Wahoo,* Walla-Walla, Wash.

I use mostly repetition of event. In *The Blossoms Meet the Vulture Lady,* it's funny when Junior is trapped in the coyote cage. It's funnier when Mud is trapped in the same coyote cage. If I could have trapped two or three more Blossoms in the coyote cage, I would have, and it would have been funnier each time.

When I was in school, the simile and the metaphor were things I encountered on English worksheets. "Find two similes and one metaphor in the second chapter of *Moby Dick.*" The rules for using similes to comic effect in children's books are, I think, the same as the rules for using metaphors: (1) Stick to the familiar and (2) Don't use them at all unless you absolutely can't stop yourself.

A simile in a children's book must be within the child's reach. The Bingo Brown books lend themselves to the simile, because the reader accepts that these are Bingo's comparisons, rather than mine. When Bingo has a mixed-sex conversation with Melissa, it's "like the Olympics of mixed-sex conversations." When he lies down on his Smurf sheets, he's "as uncomfortable as if he were lying on real Smurfs." When he takes off half his eyebrow during his first shave, the remaining eyebrow has "a suggestive snarl, like the curl of Elvis Presley's lip."

Even the best writer gets carried away by past experience. When Mark Twain has Huck describe a piece of meat as no better than "a hunk of old cold cannibal in the morning," surely he was swayed by his own travels in the Sandwich Islands, rather than by Huck's experience. I had a book as a child in which the sky of the North Pole had a gargoylelike face that blew down on the world. Because of the lingering effect of this picture — I can still see it sixty years later — I wrote a line in *The Cybil War* describing a teacher who, in her displeasure with Simon, speaks, and "It was as if the North Pole had spoken." That was not a good simile; it was self-indulgence.

We also tend to repeat our similes, possibly because we're afraid the reader might have missed one. Time and again one of Wodehouse's characters makes a noise like a dying duck. I could never imagine it — other than a sort of feeble quack — and then I read somewhere in a footnote that these rubber ducks used to be popular, and when the air went out of them, the last sound was quite comical, similar to a whoopee cushion. Certainly, it amused Wode-house everytime he thought of it. Occasionally, he varies this with a noise "like the gasp of a dying zebra," but his heart never seems to be in it.

Wodehouse was a master at building up to a simile or metaphor. In *The Butler Did It,* he describes Roscoe Bun-yan: "His face was red, the back of his neck overflowed his collar, and there had recently been published a second edition of his chin." He also invented the three-part simile, in which something is compared to three other items, the first two of which are normal, the third, exaggerated. He describes a friendship as compared to those read about in literature — "Damon and Pythias, David and Jonathan, Abercrombie and Fitch." Here's my attempt. Bingo Brown has just been grabbed around the neck by CiCi Boles, which made "Bingo feel he was the helpless victim of a force of nature, a tornado or an earthquake or one of those baboons that kill their mates by twisting off their heads."

Max Eastman compares punning to the "bodily joy of being tossed through the air toward the arms of a nice plump mother and failing to arrive." There was even a book printed in Swift's time with seventy-six rules for pun-ning, such as "Any person may pun upon another man's puns about half an hour after he has made them."

The pun is not for all of us. To be funny, a pun must be terrible. Groucho Marx made one of the worst — there-fore best — puns in *Animal Crackers.* He found when he was hunting elephants in Africa that the tusks were hard to dig out, but that "in Alabama, the Tuscaloosa."

In almost forty books, I have only one pun, and I was so pleased that I wrote a whole book to go with it. I recall the exact moment I got this pun. I had just finished reading

Alison Lurie's *War Between the Tates,* and I was wishing I could think of a clever title like that, and almost immediately, *The Cybil War* popped into my mind. I don't know if all writers get such intense pleasure out of their puns, but I typed up the title page and sat there smiling at it for some time.

Understatement is one of the funniest forms of humor, but easily lost on kids. The knack of producing humor by using understatement is to finish a sentence with a word or phrase that is milder than the listener expected, anticlimatic. Kids have an innate ability for this kind of humor and do it without even trying: "Dear Betsy, Everyone has to write a real live author and I hope you're alive or I have to write a poem."

My favorite letter was written, not to me, but to Laura Ingalls Wilder, but I used it in *The Burning Questions of Bingo Brown.* "Dear Laura Ingalls Wilder, I know that you are dead, but please write if you can and let me know where you get your ideas."

The master of finishing sentences with something incongruous, something the reader did not expect, was Kin Hubbard, who wrote the shortest newspaper column in journalistic history. Kin Hubbard could express all he wanted to say in so few words, that each of his columns consisted of one sentence. One of my favorites was, "Miss Linnet Spry was confined to her home with a swollen dresser drawer."

Supposedly, once you start defining humor, you lose it, but I don't think it would hurt to look at the origin of the word. In Latin, *humor* meant wetness, as in today's *humidity.* Then, in Hippocrates' day, it came to mean the liquid currents that flowed through the body. So a man was "out of humor" and the physician's job was to keep him in "good humor." Later, the word branched out, and one meaning — from which came our modern word — was "odd or incongruous."

This meaning is the basis for the humorous character in literature, and by "humorous character" I mean the individual in whom some particular quality is developed beyond those of his fellow man, such as Mr. Pickwick's self-forgetfulness or Don Quixote's knightly dedication. Humorous characters seem to walk off the pages and directly into our lives — Sancho, Falstaff, the Vicar of Wakefield, Jeeves, The Ruggles of Red Gap, Huckleberry Finn.

The true humorous character does not clash with reality. There has to be the element of plausibility, or the result is a comic character, which is different. I consider Mad Mary a humorous character because not only is she plausible, she is based on a real woman. But she is in no way comic.

The humor of situation arises out of confusion, mix-ups, blunders, and misadventures. Plato pointed out that we laugh at the misfortunes of others for joy that we do not share them. That may be part of it. But the humor of confusion depends more on the characters involved than the action itself. The Blossom characters came first, and the confusions befell the most vulnerable of them — Pap, Mad Mary, Ralphie, Junior, and Mud. Although confusion is a part of all the Blossoms' daily existence, it's somehow most humorous when it happens to these five.

Children need parody, just as adults do, because it is a form of humorous protest. The essential point in the use of parody, I think, is to prick a balloon, to show how ridiculous or even how painful some element of our daily lives is.

My favorite target, of course, is the *National Enquirer.* Among the headlines Bingo Brown fears to appear in are BOY LOVES TWO GIRLS FOR INFINITY, SETS WORLD RECORD; but in *The Midnight Fox,* long before I was aware of the *Enquirer,* I parodied headlines. Petie Burkis writes of a personal humiliation at a park — BOY FALLS DOWN BANK WHILE GIRL ONLOOKERS CHEER — and then goes on to write a story that sounds like it had come from a real newspaper.

TV lends itself particularly well to parody, which is one of the reasons I enjoyed writing *The TV Kid.* I relished the creation of "Give It a Spin," the game show where YOU pick your prizes and WE see that you take them, and the commercial for "Friend," the lifesize doll that allows you always to have someone to talk to. My favorite was a commercial that Lennie imagines for Fail-Ease, the tablet that eases failure and makes you less afraid to fail the next time. "Yes, for the nagging relief from failure take Fail-Ease, the failure reliever that requires no prescription." Don't we wish.

Actually, it is not I who think up these parodies. It is a character in the book, in the same way that while I could never write a country-western song, I can create a character who can write "My Angel Went to Heaven in a DC-3." I cannot write poetry, but I can create a character who, without batting an eye, can turn out complicated rhymes: "I love the roof and that's the troof."

There's a whole area of what I would call negative humor — insults, sarcasm, ridicule — hostile humor. Children, in real life, dread ridicule so much, they guard against it. If they are afraid they won't get an invitation, they say, "I wouldn't go to the party if I was invited." If scorned for sloppiness, they become twice as sloppy to show they couldn't care less.

They like insults as long as someone else is the target. Milton Berle, who should know, says the insult is popular because it boosts an audience's feeling of superiority over the object of the gag. When I needed insults in *The Burning Questions of Bingo Brown,* I got a book of insults, just as Billy Wentworth did, and I dealt them out with the same ruthlessness as he did.

"Mamie Lou, you are a perfect ten. Your face is a two, your body is a two, your legs are a two — " Mamie Lou wisely didn't wait around to hear what her other twos were.

"Harriet, you may not have invented ugliness, but you sure are the local distributor."

"Miss Fanucci is so ugly that when she goes to the zoo she has to buy two tickets — one to get in and one to get out."

Since Miss Fanucci overhears her insult, that puts a blessed end to the insults. Speaking of insults, Sinclair Lewis pointed out there are two insults that no human will endure — that he has never known trouble and that he has no sense of humor.

Nonsense is comical, and it's comical in essentially the same way to grown-ups and to children. That is not true of all humor. Nonsense has a disarming lack of pretense, and yet it requires a keen, logical mind to write nonsense which will endure. I have never — intentionally — said anything nonsensical, but one of my first loves was Uncle Wiggily. I looked forward particularly to those nonsense endings — "If the dogwood tree doesn't bark at the pussy willow and make its tail fluff up, I'll tell you about Uncle Wiggily and Nurse Fuzzywuzzy."

My father read me these books at bedtime, and when I reread them today, I still seem to hear my father's voice quicken as he got to the nonsense at the end of the chapter. It may well have been relief that he could get back to his easy chair and newspaper and Camel cigarettes, but I thought it was pleasure. And even the least of the endings is dear to me. "And if the ice cream cone doesn't jump up and down on the tablecloth, and poke holes in the loaf of bread . . ."

And my father would audibly close the book and give a three-note, down-the-scale, "Ha, ha, ha" that Pavarotti would have envied. No one could wrap up a chapter in a more satisfying way than Howard Garis and my father.

I have come across a lot of comments about humor that I like: Fred Allen's "All I know about humor is that I don't know anything about it." I thought about that as I was writing this paper, as well as the disquieting, "With notable exception, humor is written about by people who haven't any." I like Thurber's "Humor is emotional chaos remembered in tranquility."

But Stephen Leacock seemed to sum it up best.

> Humor goes on its way, moving from lower to higher forms, from cruelty to horseplay, from horseplay to wit, from wit to the higher humor of character and beyond that to its highest stage as the humor of life itself. Here, tears and laughter are joined, and our little life, incongruous and vain, is rounded with a smile.[2]

"And now if my typewriter doesn't go in swimming and get its hair ribbon all wet, so it's as crinkly as a corkscrew . . ." — I'll see you next time.

NOTES

1. Betsy Byars, *The 18th Emergency* (New York: Viking Press, 1973).
2. Stephen Leacock, *Humor and Humanity* (New York: Holt, Rinehart & Winston, 1938).